Kids-Tell-'Em Bible Stories

Active Lessons Kids Can Lead

Susan L. Lingo

STANDARD PUBLISHING

Cincinnati, Ohio

Dedication

And a little child will lead them.
Isaiah 11:6

Kids-Tell-'Em Bible Stories
©1999 Susan L. Lingo

Published by The Standard Publishing Company, Cincinnati, Ohio 45231. A division of Standex International Corporation.

Credits
Produced by Susan L. Lingo, Bright Ideas Books™
Illustrated by Marilynn G. Barr
Cover design by Liz Howe
Cover illustration by Megan Jeffery

06 05 04 03 02 01 00 99   5 4 3 2 1
ISBN 0-7847-0940-8
Printed in the United States of America

CONTENTS

INTRODUCTION

What's more fun than hearing a good story? Telling a good story!

And that's just what kids get the opportunity to do with the stories and lessons included in *Kids-Tell-'Em Bible Stories!* From puppet skits and slick story tricks to dynamite displays on the overhead projector, your children will take charge and have a ball sharing memorable Bible stories and accompanying activities with their peers. Each Bible-story lesson is a four-part adventure that several children can lead. Simply photocopy the story and lesson parts for volunteers to practice during the week. Then—voilà—memorable Bible stories and truths kids can put to use in their lives! Each simple-to-prepare Bible-story lesson includes:

✳ **Say It!** Bible stories have never been more memorable for kids! Each story is simple to prepare, exciting to tell, and has a specific theme and Scripture basis. Kids will know exactly what they're teaching!

✳ **Play It!** Every story is followed by a lively activity to support the story's theme. Sometimes a game, sometimes a craft or song, but *always* fresh, fun, and full of Bible focus.

✳ **Pray It!** Story lessons wind down with meaningful prayer activities that offer children a time to express their thoughts, feelings, and thanksgiving to God. Is anything as beautiful as watching a child lead prayer?

✳ **Replay It!** Reinforce and enrich story themes and biblical truths with these lively lesson stretchers. Use them now or save them for later!

Give your children a chance to serve others and God and help them nurture a sense of responsibility for learning with *Kids-Tell-'Em Bible Stories*—and turn "Tell me a story!" into "Let *me* tell a Bible story!"

Made by God!

Genesis 1:1–2:2; Psalm 74:17

What You'll Teach

God made the world with love.

What You'll Need

- For **Say It!** you'll need colorful markers, scissors, an overhead projector, and one clear overhead transparency. If you don't have access to an overhead, refer to the Storyteller Tips box.
- For **Play It!** you'll need paper and markers.
- For **Pray It!** you'll need a Bible.

Kid-Clue

You'll be using colorful transparencies and the overhead projector to tell the story of creation. Practice the story several times to be a super storyteller!

SAY IT!

Before class, prepare the overhead transparency as follows. Cut the transparency crosswise into four 2-by-8-inch strips and one 3-by-8-inch section. Color a green meadow or jungle scene on the large section. Add trees, flowers, and a pond. Write a number 3 in one corner to signify the third day of creation. (See illustration.) Draw Adam and Eve with several animals beside them on one of the smaller strips. Write a number 6 in the corner. On another strip, draw several birds flying in the air, then write a number 5 in the corner. On the third strip, draw a bright sun and a number 4 in the corner. On the last strip, color a blue sky with clouds and place a number 2 in the corner.

Gather kids near the overhead, but don't turn on the overhead light yet. Ask children to tell about something special they've made and why they liked it.

After several responses, say: **It's fun to make things, but we really can't create things. Only God can create. Did you know that God created something very special? And he didn't just use clay or paper and crayons to make his giant project like we do—he created everything out of nothing! Plus, God really liked all that he had made. God liked his creation because he made it with great love. What did God create? Let's find out!** Turn out the light in the room, then tell the following story.

Storyteller TIPS

If you don't have an overhead projector, use a large sheet of white poster board. Cut the poster board crosswise into five sections and follow the directions for drawing the pictures. You'll need tape to attach these story strips to the wall.

Made by God!

The Bible says that in the beginning, the world was dark and without form. Then God said, "Let there be light," and there was light! Turn on the overhead projector. **God made the light and the dark, and that was the first day of his creation. On the second day, God made air and called it the sky.** Place creation strip number 2 on the overhead so it sits at the top of the screen. **Then God created the land to separate the waters. And on the land he created trees and flowers and all sorts of fruits and grains and seeds to make more plants.** Place creation strip 3 on the overhead at the bottom of the screen. **God also saw that his creation was good. This was the third day.**

Then God created the lights in the heavens. Place creation strip 4 under the picture of the sky. **God made the moon and stars to rule the night and the sun to rule the day. This was day four. On day five, God created the birds and fish.** Place creation strip 5 below the picture of the sun. **And God saw that all his creation was good. Now what did God create on day six? Animals and people!** Place creation strip 6 on the overhead between the birds and the land. **God made them all and saw that his creation was very good indeed! God blessed the seventh day and made it holy. And finally God rested from his work.**

Turn off the overhead and ask:

- **What does God's creation tell us about him?**
- **How does God's creation show his love for us?**
- **In what ways can we thank God for our wonderful world?**

Say: **Each time we look at ourselves or others or the world of nature, we see the beauty of God's creation! Just think how much work went into creating the whole world and all the heavens. That was quite a job! Let's play a game to see how good we are at making something.**

PLAY IT!

Form seven groups and designate one group to represent each day of creation. Give each group a sheet of paper and a marker. Hand groups two through six their corresponding creation strips to look at. Then have group seven (rest) find a place to gather.

Explain that groups have 5 minutes to make up actions that describe their assigned days of creation and to write a two-line rhyme about what took place on that day. For example, day one might write, "It was dark as inky night, then God decided to make the light."

Call time after 5 minutes. Invite each group, in order of creation, to present its actions and rhyme. When everyone has had a turn, ask:

- **Was it easy to create your actions and rhymes? Explain.**
- **Do you think God put a lot of thought into his creation? Why?**

Say: **Just making up actions and rhymes was hard enough. Imagine creating the entire world and all that's in it and above it! God created the world with careful thought and loads of love! And we can thank God for his creation by taking care of the world and by thanking God in prayer.**

PRAY IT!

Invite children to stand in a circle, then point out that the circle represents the world and all that God created. Read aloud Psalm 74:17, then say: **Let's offer a prayer thanking God for all his creation. When we get to the right place, you can thank God for your favorite part of creation. Maybe it's the mountains or a favorite animal or even a little brother or sister. Let's join hands.** Pray: **Dear God, we thank you for all the love that went into your creation. We also want to thank you for ...** (fill in with the favorite parts of creation). **And God, we thank you most of all for your love. Amen.**

REPLAY IT!

Try this fun idea to reinforce and enrich the Bible lesson!

● Cut clear vinyl (found in most craft or fabric stores) into 8-inch squares. Invite children to use permanent markers to draw and color pictures of their favorite things in creation. These colorful scenes will cling to windows and give a lovely stained-glass appearance.

Noah Obeys God

Genesis 6, 7; Genesis 6:22

What You'll Teach

It's important to obey God.

What You'll Need

- For **Say It!** you'll need a Bible and a bedsheet.
- For **Play It!** you'll need index cards, tape, newsprint, and markers.
- For **Pray It!** you'll need no supplies.

Kid-Clue

You'll be using a bedsheet and lots of fun noises from the class to tell the story of how Noah obeyed God and built the ark. Practice the story several times to be a super storyteller!

SAY IT!

Hold up the bedsheet and say: **Today's Bible story is about a man named Noah and how he chose to obey God. You can help me tell the story, but first we need pairs of pretend animals—big and small to creep and crawl.** Choose pairs of kids to be elephants, lions, rabbits, kangaroos, horses, sheep, and birds. Invite each pair of ark animals to practice the appropriate animal sounds and movements. Then have the ark animals sit in pairs and listen for their cues.

Drape the bedsheet over your shoulder, then tell the following story.

Storyteller TIPS

Present this story to the adult congregation. Have adults participate in the story as special-effects soundmakers who make the sounds of Noah's tools, animals clomping, and rain pattering.

10

Noah Obeys God

Noah was a good man who loved and obeyed God in all he did. Drape the bedsheet around your face and scowl. **But the rest of the people in the world didn't love God and didn't obey him. Grrrr, they were mean!** Waggle the sheet in front of you several times. **So God decided to wash the world clean with a huge flood—but God promised to save Noah and his family.** Drape the sheet over your shoulder. **God told Noah to build an ark. Let's make the sounds of Noah's tools. Noah chopped wood** (make chopping sounds with your hands on your knees), **Noah sawed** (make sawing sound and motions), **and Noah hammered** (hammer on the floor with your fists). **Noah obeyed God and built the ark. Yeah, Noah!** Lead everyone in clapping.

Scrunch the bedsheet in a long pile on the ground, being sure to keep the edge of the sheet on top. **When Noah's ark was finished, God called the animals to come in pairs. Here come the elephants!** Have the elephants come to the ark making elephant noises. Have the elephants stand behind the sheet. **Then came the lions** (pause for the lions to come) **and the rabbits** (pause) **and the kangaroos** (pause) **and the horses** (pause) **and the sheep** (pause) **and finally the birds. When everyone was safe in the ark, God closed the door—whump!** Clap your hands one time. **Then it began to rain.** Pat your knees to make the sound of falling rain. Hold the edge of the sheet and begin pulling it up little by little to make the rising flood. **As the rain came down, the flood waters came up.** Hold the bedsheet about halfway up, then begin to gently move it back and forth. **The ark sailed back and forth on the water, and all the animals swayed back and forth, back and forth. But they were safe! Why? Because Noah had obeyed God!**

After many months, God made a wind blow across the water (make blowing noises), **and the flood water went down, down, down** (lower the sheet slowly, then set it on the floor) **until the ark came to rest on a mountain. Noah sent birds to fly away and find dry land.** Instruct the birds to fly from the ark. **When the birds didn't come back, the door to the ark was opened and Noah and his family and all the animals came out. What a parade it was!** Have the pretend animals make noises as they leave the ark. Then have them sit on the floor. **Everyone was glad to be safe and sound. And everyone was especially glad that Noah had obeyed God! Yeah, Noah!** Lead everyone in clapping.

Set the bedsheet aside, then ask:
- **Why did Noah choose to obey God?**
- **What might have happened if Noah hadn't obeyed God?**
- **How is obeying God a good way to show we love him?**
- **How can we obey God in all we do?**

Say: **Let's learn more about obeying God by reading from the Bible.** Read aloud Genesis 6:22, then say: **Just as Noah obeyed God in all he did, we can obey God too. Let's sing a lively song to remind us how important it is to obey God.**

PLAY IT!

Before this activity, write the words to the rhythm rap below on newsprint and tape it to the wall so kids can read the words. Then hand each person four index cards and a marker. Tell kids to spell the word "obey" by writing one letter of the word on each card. Say: **Noah might have called God *Yahweh* when he asked God's help in being obedient. But whether we call him God or Yahweh, it's important to obey him all the time. Let's rap out a cool rhyme that will help us remember to obey God. As we say the words, follow me in the motions and hold up your letter cards at the start of each line in the chorus to spell out the word obey.**

Begin by slowly repeating the rap in a fun rhythm so kids become familiar with the words and beat. Then add the motions and the letter cards as you speed up the rhythm. Repeat the rhythm rap several times.

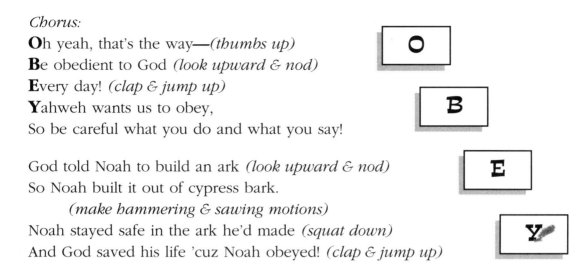

Chorus:
Oh yeah, that's the way—*(thumbs up)*
Be obedient to God *(look upward & nod)*
Every day! *(clap & jump up)*
Yahweh wants us to obey,
So be careful what you do and what you say!

God told Noah to build an ark *(look upward & nod)*
So Noah built it out of cypress bark.
        (make hammering & sawing motions)
Noah stayed safe in the ark he'd made *(squat down)*
And God saved his life 'cuz Noah obeyed! *(clap & jump up)*

Repeat chorus

Say: **Let's end with a prayer asking God to help us obey him in all we say and do. Keep holding your letter cards.**

PRAY IT!

Have children form a standing circle, holding their letter cards. Hold up each letter as you say the following prayer. **Dear God, we're thankful that Noah loved you and obeyed you. Please help us obey** (hold up the letter O card) **better** (B card) **every day** (E card). **Amen—and yes!** (Y card). Say: **We can obey better every day, yes! All we have to do is ask God to help us. Take home your letter cards to help you remember to obey God better every day—yes!**

REPLAY IT!

To reinforce and enrich the lesson, try this!

● Read aloud Genesis 6:22 again. Then brainstorm with the class a list of things we can do to obey God, such as being kind to each other, following Jesus, and respecting our parents. Copy each way to obey God onto an index card. Hand each child an index card and challenge him to obey God in that area all week. Bring the cards next week so kids can exchange them with each other.

A Heavenly Promise

Genesis 21:1-7; 2 Peter 3:9

What You'll Teach

God always keeps his promises.

What You'll Need

- For **Say It!** you'll need a Bible, construction paper, scissors, a marker, tape, and an apron. You can make a paper apron by cutting the bottom from a paper sack, then taping yarn around one of the long edges to make a waist-tie.
- For **Play It!** you'll need no supplies.
- For **Pray It!** you'll need markers and paper stars.

Kid-Clue

You'll be using paper stars and an apron with lots of pockets to tell the story of God's promise to Abram. Practice the story several times to be a super storyteller!

SAY IT!

To make a story apron, cut five 6-inch squares from construction paper, then tape the squares to the front of the apron to make pockets. Remember to leave the top edge of each pocket open! Number the pockets 1 through 5.

Then cut out twenty paper stars. (See the Storyteller Tips box for a great idea!) Make the stars at least 5 inches across. Draw a smiling face on one point of three stars. Two of the smiling stars will be Abraham and Sarah, so write their names on the backs of the stars. Fold the arms of the last smiling star inward toward the center. This will be the baby Isaac star and should look like a baby folded in his blanket. Draw faces on three more stars for the special visitors, and make one star look like a sheep. (See illustration.) Place the Abraham star in pocket 1, the Sarah star in pocket 2, the sheep star in pocket 3, the three visitors in pocket 4, and the baby Isaac star in pocket 5. (As you tell the story, pull the stars from the pockets at the appropriate times and place them on the floor or tape them to a wall.) Hide the remainder of the stars in easy-to-find places.

Tie the story apron around your waist and gather listeners in front of you. Ask them to tell about promises they've made and kept or times someone broke a promise. Then say: **God makes promises too. And even though we may forget and break our promises, God never breaks his promises! Let's hear a story about a time God made a special promise. We'll use the story apron to help.**

A Heavenly Promise

Once there was an old man who loved God very much. His name was Abram. Pull the Abraham star out of pocket 1. **Abram loved and obeyed God his entire life, and God loved Abram too. Abram had a pretty wife named Sarai.** Pull the Sarah star from pocket 2. Hold the star up, then place it in front of you or tape it to a wall. **But Abram and Sarai were sad. They didn't have any children, and they wanted a child to love so much!**

One night, God spoke to Abram. God told Abram to look up in the night sky. What do you think Abram saw? Stars! Millions and billions of twinkly stars! Then God made Abram a promise. God promised Abram that he would be the father of many nations and that his children would be more than the stars in the sky! How many is that? Let's see how many stars you can find! Tell children to search for hidden stars around the room. When all thirteen stars are found, have children return to their places.

Then God changed Abram's name to Abraham, which means "father of many," and Sarai's name to Sarah. God also

promised them a baby boy. But Abraham and Sarah were so old! Could they really have a baby? Let's see!

After a time, Abraham was watching his sheep from his tent (take the sheep star from pocket 3), **when all of a sudden three special visitors appeared.** (Remove the three stars from pocket 4.) **They told Abraham that Sarah would soon have a baby. What do you think Sarah did when she heard this? She laughed!** Invite kids to laugh, then say: **Sarah was 90 years old, and she thought she was too old for a baby. But is anything impossible for God? No! Does God always keep his promises? Yes! Soon afterward, Sarah gave birth to a baby boy.** (Remove the baby Isaac star from pocket 5.) **They named the baby Isaac, which means laughter. Then they praised God for always keeping his promises!**

Set the stars aside and ask:
- **Why do you think God always keeps his promises?**
- **Does God want us to honor our promises too? Explain.**
- **How does knowing that God keeps his promises strengthen our faith?**

Say: **Let's learn more about God's promises by reading from the Bible.** Read aloud 2 Peter 3:9a, then say: **We can trust God to always keep his promises. Now let's learn more about God's promises by playing a game called Star Stance.**

PLAY IT!

Form a standing circle and have children hold their arms out to their sides. Instruct kids to spread their feet apart and to lock elbows with their neighbors. Point out how children look like stars in a strong, locked circle. Challenge kids to keep the links strong by holding tightly to the elbows, then leaning backward. As kids lean, say: **This is a strong circle made up of strong stars. When the links stay unbroken, our circle stands strong! Now lean forward.** As kids lean in, say: **We couldn't do this without trusting each star in our circle to keep an unbroken hold. If one person broke the trust, our whole circle would collapse! Now let's try this hard trick! Let's have one person lean in, the next person lean out, and the next lean in all around the circle.** Remind children not to break the links!

Have everyone return to an upright position, then sit in place. Say: **Star Stance takes a lot of trust to keep things strong and whole. Keeping promises is the** same way. When we make a promise, we don't want it to be broken or no one will trust our word. God never breaks his promises, so we can trust the strength of his Word!

Say: **Let's end with a prayer thanking God for his promises and asking his help in always keeping our word too.**

PRAY IT!

Hand each person a marker and a paper star from *Say It!* Cut more stars if needed. Say: **Many wonderful things happen when God keeps his promises. We develop trust and assurance in God's Word, we strengthen our faith, and we respect God with a sincere heart. Let's list the things God's promises do for us on these paper stars. Write the word *strength* on one point. On the next point, write the word *trust*. Then write the word *assurance* on the next point, the word *respect* on the next point, and the word *sincerity* on the last point. If you put the first letters of these words together, you have the word *stars*. Now let's say a prayer thanking God for his loving promises that shine in our hearts like stars**.

Pray: **Dear God, thank you for loving us and for keeping your promises unbroken. It feels so good to trust in you all the time! Please help us keep our word too. Amen.** Say: **Now take your stars home to remind you that God always keeps his promises—and that you can too!**

REPLAY IT!

Try this great idea to reinforce and enrich today's lesson!

● Make sparkly stars by bending chenille wires into star shapes. Tie each star to fishing line, then tie the other end of the fishing line to the center of a pencil. Have an adult fill several large jars with boiling water. In each jar, stir 3 cups of borax (available at grocery stores) and enough blue food coloring to color the liquid. Lay three pencils across the mouth of each jar so the stars are suspended in the liquid. Set the jars aside to cool for a day. As the liquid cools, crystals will form on the stars. Remove the stars and let them drip dry. Then hang the stars in windows as beautiful sun catchers.

Red Sea Escape!

Exodus 13:20–15:18; Psalm 121

What You'll Teach

We can trust God to help us.

What You'll Need

- For **Say It!** you'll need a Bible and an old bedsheet or blanket.
- For **Play It!** you'll need a playground ball and a bedsheet.
- For **Pray It!** you'll need a Bible.

Kid-Clue

You'll be using a bedsheet to tell the story of God's people crossing the Red Sea. Practice the story several times to be a super storyteller!

SAY IT!

Set the bedsheet beside you and ask children to tell about times they've needed someone's help and how it felt to receive assistance. Then say: **God is ready to help us, and none of our troubles are too big or small for God to help with. Moses and God's people, the Israelites, learned just how wonderful and life-saving God's help can be! Let's listen to a Bible story about the time God helped his people in a big watery way. We'll use this bedsheet to help tell the story.**

Storyteller TIPS

Use a yardstick as Moses' staff or walking stick as you tell the story! You may enjoy walking across blue celophane paper for a more realistic effect.

18

Red Sea Escape!

God's people had been kept as slaves in a land called Egypt. Spread the sheet on the floor and have everyone stand around it. **Pharaoh was the mean king of Egypt. He forced the Israelites to make bricks in the hot sun. They made the bricks, they lifted the piles, and they carried the bricks—ugh!** Lead everyone in bending down to make pretend bricks, then walking around the edge of the bedsheet pretending to haul heavy bricks. Continue walking as you say: **All day in the blazing sun, God's people worked for the mean pharaoh. They needed God's help, but how would God set them free?**

Wrap the sheet around you as a robe. **God had a plan. God chose Moses to lead his people to freedom. God forced Pharaoh to let the Israelites go, and Moses led them out of Egypt.** Begin a parade around the room with the children following behind.

God showed Moses and the Israelites the way to go, so they marched and marched. In the daytime, God sent a pillar of cloud to lead them, and at night, God sent a pillar of fire. On and on they walked until . . . (pause and pretend to listen) **wait! What's that noise?** (Look behind you and point.) **Soldiers are coming! Pharaoh sent his soldiers after God's people to capture them. We must run!**

Lead the children on a jog around the room one time, then abruptly stop. Say: **Oh my, how can it be? We're trapped in our place by the mighty Red Sea!** Spread the bedsheet on the floor. **God's people were afraid. The mean soldiers were coming behind them, and in front of them lay the sea! What would they do? God heard their prayers and felt their fear—and God helped them in a miraculous way. God told Moses to lift his walking stick in the air.** (Hold your arm or yardstick in the air.)

Then God parted the Red Sea—whoosh! And God's people walked across safely. Lead children across the bedsheet, then say: **When all of God's people were safely on the other side, God closed the sea and made it whole—and Pharaoh's soldiers vanished in a whoosh!** Quickly gather up the sheet and drape it over your shoulder. Say: **God's people were safe! Then Moses and the Israelites praised and thanked God for his help!**

Spread the bedsheet on the floor and invite everyone to sit on it. Ask:

● **In what ways does God's help show his love for us?**

● **How did Moses and the Israelites respond to God's help?**

● **How can we thank God for his help in our lives?**

Say: **Let's learn more about God's help from the Bible.** Read aloud Psalm 121:1, 2. Say: **God helps us because he loves us. And even when it seems like our troubles are too big, we can trust that God is bigger than anyone or anything! Let's play a game and see if we can offer a bit of our own help.**

PLAY IT!

Form four teams and have each team stand and hold an edge of the bedsheet. Toss a ball in the center of the sheet. Explain that teams are to try to roll or bounce the ball by lifting the bedsheet in the air. The object of this game is to not let the ball touch your hands or arms. When players are tagged, they can sit beneath the sheet and poke the ball as it rolls above. Challenge kids to help each other keep the ball from tagging their team members! Play continues until one team has lost all its players.

After several games, place the sheet on the floor and sit down. Say: **That was fun! And it was fun to help our team members keep from being tagged, even if we weren't always able to do so. I'm so glad that God can help us and**

that nothing is too big or troublesome to stop him! Let's end with a prayer thanking God for his help in our lives.

PRAY IT!

Open the Bible to Psalm 121, then say: **One way to thank God is by quietly thinking about his Word and by reading from the Bible. I'd like volunteers to read from the Bible with me. As we read, think about God's loving help and all he does for us.**

Ask several volunteers to help you read. Take turns reading verses slowly and prayerfully. When the psalm has been read, quietly say: **Think about one thing in your life you need God's help for.** Pause. **Now quietly ask God for his help and end by expressing your thanks and love.** After a moment of silence, say "amen." Close by saying: **As you go through your days and nights, remember that God's help is with you because God is with you and loves you!**

REPLAY IT!

For lesson reinforcement and enrichment, try this tasty treat!

● Invite another class to share your special story, then serve Red Sea Sodas and Staffs. To make a Red Sea Soda, fill a paper cup or drinking glass with milk, then stir in 2 tablespoons of presweetened cherry Kool-Aid. Add a red licorice staff and have kids bite off the ends so they can sip through it!

God's Ten Rules

Deuteronomy 5:6-21; Psalm 24:4, 5

What You'll Teach

God gave us rules to help us.

What You'll Need

- For **Say It!** you'll need scissors, a brown marker, tape, and two large sheets of brown poster board.
- For **Play It!** you'll need a ball.
- For **Pray It!** you'll need a Bible.

Kid-Clue

You'll be using large puzzle pieces to tell the story of the Ten Commandments. Practice the story several times to be a super storyteller!

SAY IT!

Before class, cut the poster board into two big stone tablets, then cut each tablet into five large puzzle pieces. (See illustration.) Put the pieces back together and write one of the following commandments on each piece. Write commands 1 through 5 on the pieces for one stone and commands 6 through 10 on the other pieces.

1. There is only one God.
2. Don't make false idols.
3. Don't use my name in bad ways.

There is only one God.

Don't make false idols.

Don't use my name in bad ways.

Keep the Sabbath holy.

Honor your mother and father.

Don't commit murder.

Be true to your husband or wife.

Don't steal.

Don't lie.

Don't wish for other people's things.

4. Keep the Sabbath holy.

5. Honor your mother and father.

6. Don't commit murder.

7. Be true to your husband or wife.

8. Don't steal.

9. Don't lie.

10. Don't wish for other people's things.

Tell this story next to a wall, door, or bulletin board. Place the puzzle pieces on the floor with the tape. Have everyone gather around and ask them to tell about special rules they might have at home, school, or in the community. Then say: **Did you know that God has special rules for us too? Today we'll hear how Moses was first given God's special rules, called commandments. You can help tell the story. Just follow along when I give you directions.**

God's Ten Rules

A long time ago, Moses and God's people, the Israelites, made a journey. Moses and the Israelites walked and walked for many days (have children march around the room) **and finally came to Mount Sinai, the biggest mountain in that area. God had told Moses to go to Mount Sinai, so Moses and the people set down their things and camped there.** Invite children to sit in a circle.

One day God's people heard the roar of thunder and saw bolts of lightning and a thick cloud at the top of the mountain. Encourage kids to look up. **The people were terribly afraid. What could this mean?** Invite children to tell their ideas. **God was calling Moses to the top of the mountain so he could give Moses something very special. What do you think God wanted to give Moses?** Allow kids to share their ideas, then say: **God gave Moses two stone tablets. On them, God had written special rules to help Moses and the Israelites. God wanted everyone to obey the special rules. But what are they? Let's see!**

Stand beside the wall and hold the tape. Direct kids to form pairs and choose one partner to be the reader and one to be the teller. Invite one set of partners to come forward and have the reader tape the puzzle piece for the first commandment to the wall and read the commandment aloud. Then have the teller explain what the commandment means. Finally, have everyone tell why it's important to obey this commandment and what could happen if we disobey. Continue assembling the commandment puzzle pieces on the wall and discussing them until all ten are in place. When both tablets are assembled, read the Ten Commandments aloud together.

Then say: **God gave us his commandments to help keep us safe and happy and living the way he wants us to.** Ask:

● **How do God's commandments keep us safe? happy? close to God?**
● **In what ways does obeying God's rules show that we love him?**
● **How can we obey God's rules more carefully?**

Say: **Let's learn more about God's special rules by playing a game.**

PLAY IT!

Have children sit in a circle. Hold the ball and say: **In this game, we'll begin with one simple rule. You must roll the ball.** Roll the ball to someone and continue rolling the ball around the circle for a minute or two. Then say: **That was pretty easy, wasn't it? Now let's add a fun twist. Each time the ball is rolled to you, you can make up a new rule to add to my rule. For example, the new rule might be "bounce the ball one time." Then we would roll the ball and bounce it one time before rolling it again. Let's see how many rules we can add and still obey!**

Roll the ball and continue adding new rules. Play until there are too many rules to remember or obey. Then stop and discuss why it was easy to play with a few rules but hard to play with many rules. Point out that God could have given us hundreds of rules, but he chose the Ten Commandments very carefully so we could remember (and obey) them.

Play once more but limit the rules to three carefully chosen rules. Then say: **That was fun! Too many rules are hard to remember and follow. I'm glad that God gave us just ten very important commandments to obey—yes**! Have children give each other high fives. Say: **Let's end with a prayer asking for God's help in obeying him.** Set the ball aside.

PRAY IT!

Open the Bible to Psalm 24:4, 5 and ask for a volunteer to read the passage aloud. Then say: **We can trust God to care for us, and we can trust God's rules to help us if we obey them. Let's pray. Dear God, thank you for loving us enough to give us important rules to live by. Please help us study and learn your commands, and help us obey you in all that we do. Amen.**

REPLAY IT!

Try one of these fun ideas to reinforce or enrich the lesson!

● Cut pretend stone tablets from fine-grained sandpaper. Then use a brown marker to write the Ten Commandments on the stones, five to each stone. Glue the tablets to real stones and use them as paperweights.

● Leave the paper tablets on the wall. Have kids sit in a circle and roll the ball back and forth. Have kids name a commandment before they roll the ball to someone else. Challenge kids to name the commandments in order to see how well they do with only a few peeks at the wall!

Faith and Courage!

Joshua 2; Hebrews 11:1

What You'll Teach

Strong faith makes us courageous.

What You'll Need

- For **Say It!** you'll need a Bible, masking tape, scissors, rubber bands, and three 12-inch lengths of thick red yarn for each child.
- For **Play It!** you'll need a 20-foot length of red yarn.
- For **Pray It!** you'll need twist-tie wires, a hole punch, index cards, and markers.

Kid-Clue

You'll have everyone braiding red cords as you tell the story of Rahab and the spies. Practice the story (and your braiding) several times to be a super storyteller!

SAY IT!

Before the story, join three lengths of yarn at one end with a rubber band. Tape the yarn to a wall, bulletin board, or door. Hand each child three lengths of yarn and two rubber bands. Show children how to join the ends of the yarn with one of their rubber bands. Then ask:

- **When is a time you felt brave?**
- **Who helps us be brave?**

Say: **Today we'll learn that faith in God helps us be brave. We'll learn about a woman named Rahab and how she helped God's soldiers. As you listen to the story, you'll be braiding special red cords like the one Rahab used. Now find a partner who knows how to braid.** Pause, then demonstrate how to tape the rubber bands to the floor or to kids' shoes. Have children hold the three strands of yarn apart. Say: **Every time you hear the word _right,_ bring the piece of yarn on the far right over to lie between the other two pieces of yarn, like this.** Use your yarn to demonstrate how to do this. **When you hear the word _left,_ bring the piece of yarn on the far left over to lie between the other two pieces, like this.** Demonstrate using your yarn. **Hold your yarn to keep it tight as you braid. Now let's hear the story of brave Rahab!**

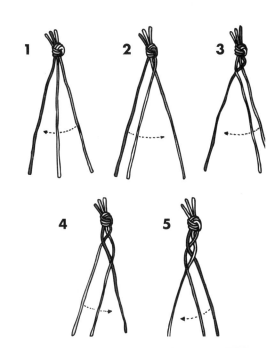

Faith and Courage!

Joshua and God's other soldiers were _right_ outside the city of Jericho. God wanted his people to conquer the city, but there was one big problem. A huge wall went around the city. The wall went as far to the _left_ as they could see. The wall went as far to the _right_ as they could see. How could God's soldiers get over that wall? Joshua sent two spies to check out the city and its wall. The spies _left_ and came _right_ to the house of a woman named Rahab.

The mean king of Jericho heard that Rahab was hiding two of God's spies, and he was angry. "Find those spies!" he told his men, so they _left_ to find them. Now Rahab had only heard about God's power, but she had faith in all God could do. So Rahab hid God's spies _right_ on her roof! She hid them under some grain _left_ over from the harvest. Oh, Rahab! What a brave thing to do!

When the king's men came to Rahab, she told them to hurry _right_ away—maybe they'd catch the spies. When the king's men _left,_ Rahab told God's soldiers, "Our people have heard about the great power of your God. I know that God has

Storyteller TIPS

• Be sure to pause after you say "left" and "right" so everyone can keep up with their braiding.

• Use an overhead projector to help tell the story. Simply tape the strands of yarn to the surface of the projector, then do your braiding on the glass plate so everyone can see and follow along.

given you this land. Now *right* before you go, promise before God that you will be kind and let my family live, for I have been kind to you! The spies promised that God would spare their lives if Rahab told no one they'd been there. Then Rahab tossed a red cord out her window and the spies *left* to escape.

Because of Rahab's faith in God's power, she courageously helped the spies. And when God's soldiers fought Jericho, God told them to spare the lives of Rahab and her family. *Right* on, Rahab!

Have children use their second rubber bands to tie the ends of their braids. Set the braids aside, then say: **The Bible tells us that Rahab saved herself and her family through her faith in God. Hebrews 11:31 says that by faith, Rahab welcomed God's spies and was not killed with those who refused to obey God.** Ask:

● **How does faith in God help us be brave and courageous?**
● **Why do you think God wants our faith to be strong?**
● **What kinds of things can we do when we have strong, courageous faith?**

Read aloud Hebrews 11:1, then say: **Even though Rahab had only heard of God, she had faith in his awesome power. And that faith helped her act in a courageous way. Let's use a red cord like Rahab's to play a lively game that will remind us of ways to strengthen our faith.**

PLAY IT!

Place the 20-foot length of yarn in a large circle on the ground and have children sit just inside the yarn circle. Choose one person to be a spy and have the spy hold one of the braids made during the story time. Explain that the spy will walk around the circle with the red cord. When the braided cord is dropped in front of someone, that person must chase the spy back to the open place in the circle. When the spy reaches the space, she must then tell one way to strengthen our faith, such as through prayer, reading the Bible, or helping others. If the spy is tagged before sitting down in the circle, she remains a spy for another turn. Play until everyone has been either a spy or a chaser.

After the game, say: **Rahab's faith grew when she helped God's spies, and her faith grew again when God spared her life. It's important to strengthen our faith and to keep it growing. Let's end with a prayer asking God to help us look for ways to strengthen our faith in him.**

28

PRAY IT!

Have children hold the braided cords they made during *Say It!* Give each child an index card and marker, then have kids write the words to Hebrews 11:1 on the cards. (You may wish to write the verse on a sheet of newsprint and hang it on the wall for everyone to see.) When the verses are written, punch a hole in the top center of each card, then use a twist-tie wire to attach the card to the braid. Finally, invite everyone to stand in a circle and have children gently hold the braids of the people next to them.

Say: **Just as the yarn in our cords is joined, we can join together in prayer. Let's bow our heads and ask for God's help in strengthening our faith.** Pray: **Dear God, thank you for your power, might, and love. Please help us grow stronger in our faith so that we can bravely serve you and courageously help others. In Jesus' name, amen.**

Take your red cord home and hang it on a wall or door to remind you of Rahab and her courageous spirit for God. The red cord will also remind you that when your faith in God is strong, so is your courage!

REPLAY IT!

Use this fun idea to reinforce and enrich the Bible lesson!

● As a service project, have children use the cord from *Play It!* to make 6-inch red braids to use as Bible bookmarks. Secure the ends of each braid with rubber bands, then add a small card with Hebrews 11:1 written on it. Tie curling ribbon around the rubber band at the top of the braid. Present the special bookmarks to another class or to the adult congregation.

Whatta Wall!

Joshua 6; Jeremiah 29:11

What You'll Teach

God has a plan for your life.

What You'll Need

- For **Say It!** you'll need black markers, brown paper grocery sacks, clear packing tape, scissors, and a large box. Be sure the large box is big enough to wear as a costume!
- For **Play It!** you'll need a Bible, paper plates, tape, and a small prize for each player. Prizes could include wrapped candies, erasers, or pencils.
- For **Pray It!** you'll need a Bible, scissors, old blueprints (available from architects or house builders), tape, pencils, and red and pink construction paper.

Kid-Clue

You'll tell the story of Jericho by pretending to be a part of a brick wall. Practice several times to be a super storyteller!

SAY IT!

Before class, you'll need to make a simple costume that looks like a brick wall. Cover a large box with brown paper grocery sacks, then use a marker to add brick lines. Cut the flaps from one end of the large box. Cut a hole in the front of the large box for your head to fit through. Then cut arm holes in the sides or front edges of the large box. (See illustration.) Now try on your costume and—voilà—you've become a nifty brick wall!

Storyteller TIPS

Have a friend grab a box and become a brick wall too. Divide the Bible story into parts and you'll have twice the fun!

30

Put on your costume and gather children in a group. Present the following skit and story, inviting kids to play active roles at your direction.

Whatta Wall!

Say: **Hello—my name's Wally, and I'm a brick wall.** Pat your sides. **Being a wall isn't the easiest thing in the world, you know! It's hard work standing in place for years and years in the hot sun and the freezing snow—brrrr!** Make the box shake and rattle. **Yep, it's not easy being a wall, but it can be exciting—wahoo!** Comically kick up your heels. **Let me tell you about the most exciting time I ever had. It was a long. long time ago and I had an important job to do. I stretched and wound my way all around the city of Jericho. I was over 20 feet tall and 20 feet wide, and God's soldiers couldn't get over me. But their leader's name was Joshua, and he was very wise. Joshua loved God and knew that God had a plan to get his soldiers into the city.** Shake your finger. **Oh, Jericho was a bad city where people were mean to each other and didn't love God. God wanted his own people to have Jericho—but I was so big!** Jump up and down. **They'd never climb over me! But God had a plan!**

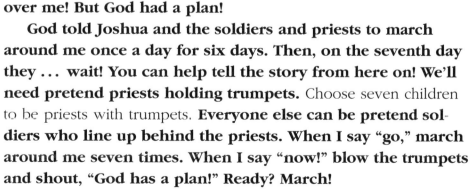

God told Joshua and the soldiers and priests to march around me once a day for six days. Then, on the seventh day they ... wait! You can help tell the story from here on! We'll need pretend priests holding trumpets. Choose seven children to be priests with trumpets. **Everyone else can be pretend soldiers who line up behind the priests. When I say "go," march around me seven times. When I say "now!" blow the trumpets and shout, "God has a plan!" Ready? March!**

When everyone has circled you seven times, shout "now!" then carefully fall down and lie on the floor. Say: **Whoa! That's what**

happened when everyone obeyed God's plan! I came tumbling down, and God's people rushed into the city. Pretty awesome, eh? Flail around a bit, then say: **Hey! Can someone help me up? Brick walls need a little help now and then, you know.** When upright, say: **Thanks! That was an exciting story. God planned for Joshua to lead his people. God planned the way to bring down the big wall. God planned for his people to take over Jericho. And God has a plan for our lives too! Just remember:**

   God has a plan if we'll just obey.

   God guides our lives each step of the way! See ya! Wave good-bye as you exit.

After you exit, have someone ask these story questions:
- **Why is it important to obey God's plans?**
- **How does having faith and trust help us obey God?**
- **What do you think God's plans are for you?**

Then say: **Let's plan our moves in an exciting game to remind us that God makes the perfect plans for our lives.**

PLAY IT!

Tape twenty-five paper plates in a grid as shown in the illustration. Be sure the plates are 6 to 8 inches apart. Line the prizes up 1 foot away from one end of the grid.

Have children form pairs, then direct each pair to stand on a paper plate at the end opposite the prizes. Instruct partners to link elbows. Explain that they need to plan a way to get to the prizes by taking four hops to different paper plates. Allow several moments of planning, then invite two pairs to begin carrying out their plans. When all the pairs have had a chance to collect their prizes, discuss why plans are important to goals. Then have partners tell each other why God's plans are important in their lives and how they can obey his plans better.

Read aloud Jeremiah 29:11, then say: **God is wiser than anyone, and he knows the plans he has set out for us. God's plans for us give us hope and joy! Now let's thank God for his wonderful plans for our lives.**

PRAY IT!

Before class, cut a 3-inch heart shape for each child from red or pink constuction paper. Cut a 3-by-8-inch piece of blueprint paper for each child.

Read aloud Jeremiah 29:11 from the Bible, then say: **God has special plans for us. God has a plan to prosper us, which means God will help us have what we need. God has a plan to help us—not harm us. And God has plans to give us hope and a good future.** Ask:

- **Why is it important to trust in God's plans?**
- **How can obeying God help accomplish his plans for us?**
- **How do God's plans show his love for us?**

Hand each child a paper heart and a pencil. Have children write "For I know the plans I have for you" on one side of their paper hearts. Then invite children to form four groups and designate each group to pray and thank God for a particular plan mentioned in the verse. Have them write that plan on the backs of their paper hearts. For example, invite one group to quietly thank God for his plan to prosper us and write the word "prosper" on the backs of their paper hearts. Ask another group to pray for God's plan to give us a future, then write the word "future" on the backs of their hearts.

When you've prayed, hand everyone a piece of blueprint paper. Say: **Following blueprints helps us know how to construct buildings. In the same way, God helps us construct our lives when we follow his plans. Tape the heart-shaped verse to one end of your blueprint to make a bookmark that will remind you that God has a plan for your life.** Encourage children to mark Jeremiah 29:11 with their bookmarks and challenge them to read the verse each day for a week.

REPLAY IT!

For lesson reinforcement and enrichment, try this fun idea!

- Invite kids to make horns to blow during the retelling of the story of Joshua at Jericho. Buy inexpensive plastic funnels from a hardware store and decorate them with permanent markers or paint pens. Attach thin paper over the wide end with a rubber band, then hum through the small opening—your trumpet will sound like a kazoo!

Fabulous Friends

Ruth 1, 2; Ecclesiastes 4:10

What You'll Teach

God gives us good friends.

What You'll Need

- For **Say It!** you'll need a Bible, permanent markers, and a bag of balloons.
- For **Play It!** you'll need a balloon for each person.
- For **Pray It!** you'll need markers and the balloons from *Play It!*

Kid-Clue

You'll pass balloons around a circle as you tell the story of Ruth and Naomi. Practice the story several times to be a super storyteller!

SAY IT!

Before class, inflate seven balloons. Draw three balloons with women's faces and four balloons with men's faces. Write one each of these names on the women's balloons: Naomi, Ruth, and Orpah. Write the name Boaz on one of the men's balloons. Inflate an eighth balloon, but make it very small. Draw a smiling baby face on the balloon.

Have kids stand in a circle. Place the balloons on the floor beside you. As you tell the story of Ruth and Naomi, gently pass the character balloons around the circle, adding them in or taking them out as the story continues. Begin by asking: **Do you have a very good friend? Did you know**

Storyteller TIPS

You may want to use pink balloons for the women story characters and blue balloons for the men. For added fun, bop the balloons around the circle instead of passing them.

that God gives us good friends? Today we'll hear a story about two women who were very good friends. **Ruth was a young woman** (hold up the Ruth balloon), **and Naomi was her older friend** (hold up the Naomi balloon). **As I tell the story of Ruth and Naomi, we'll pass the balloons back and forth.**

Fabulous Friends

Once there was a woman named Naomi. Begin passing the Naomi balloon. **Naomi had a husband** (pass one of the men balloons) **and two fine sons.** Add in two more men balloons. **Naomi and her family loved God and lived in Bethlehem. One day, the family moved to a placed called Moab, where no one knew God. The sons married two young women. Their names were Ruth** (pass the Ruth balloon) **and Orpah.** Pass the Orpah balloon. **Naomi loved Ruth and Orpah and told them about God.**

After many years, Naomi's husband and sons died. Set aside the three men balloons. **Naomi, Ruth, and Orpah were left alone. Naomi wanted Ruth and Orpah to go back to their families, so Orpah sadly left.** Set aside the Orpah balloon. **But did Ruth go? Oh no! Ruth loved Naomi and wanted to stay with her. Ruth and Naomi both loved God, and they knew God gives us good friends. So Ruth went with Naomi back to Bethlehem.**

In Bethlehem, there was a wealthy man named Boaz. Add in the Boaz balloon. **Boaz noticed Ruth working hard in the fields. Boaz was kind to Ruth and gave her grain to share with Naomi. One day, Boaz asked Ruth to marry him. Naomi was so happy for her friend! Boaz and Ruth were married and took care of Naomi. Then one day, Ruth and Boaz had a baby.** Add in the baby balloon. **And who do you think was the happiest of all? Ruth's best friend, Naomi!**

Set the balloons aside, then ask:

- **How did Naomi's telling Ruth about God bring the two friends even closer?**
- **How are friends one way God shows his love for us?**
- **In what ways can we help our friends?**

Say: **Let's learn more about being friends by reading from the Bible.** Read aloud Ruth 1:16 and Ecclesiastes 4:10, then say: **Good friends help each other, have fun together, and encourage one another. Let's play a game with our friends to remember that friends are special gifts from God.**

PLAY IT!

Hand each child a balloon to inflate and tie off. Form groups of five or six. Have each group choose one person to be the balloon starter and place the balloons on the floor next to that person.

Say: **In this game, friends will help friends pass the balloons. Start by passing one balloon to someone in your group and tell him or her your name. Remember who you passed the balloon to! Then have that person pass the balloon and repeat his or her name and so on. After a few passes, start passing another balloon in the same pattern. Keep adding balloons and passing them in the same pattern until all the balloons are in play. If a balloon is dropped or someone gets mixed up, your friends can help!**

After several minutes of passing, encourage kids to try a little balloon acceleration and pass the balloons faster. After several more minutes, have each group join with another to make a huge circle of friends, then begin passing the balloons to new friends.

End the game by having children sit down in their groups and passing the balloons several more times around the circle. Then say: **Friends have great times together, don't they? You know, sometimes we forget to thank God for our friends. We may even forget to include friends in our prayers. Let's end with a prayer thanking God for good friends.**

PRAY IT!

Be sure everyone has a balloon. Distribute the markers and challenge kids to draw the face of a friend on their balloons. Have children write their friends' first names on the backs of the balloons. Then say: **Take a moment to think about this friend. Think about the good times you've shared, and remember the help your friend has given you along with all the smiles and laughter. Think about how good God was to give you this friend. Now think about one thing you could pray for your friend. Silently think of that need during our prayer as you hold your balloon.** Pray: **Dear God, thank you for the friends you give us. Help us be good friends in return. Please help my friend in this way.** Pause. **And thank you, God, for being our best friend. Amen.**

Take your balloon home to give to your friend or to keep in your room as a reminder to pray and thank God for your good friend.

REPLAY IT!

For reinforcement and enrichment, try one of these fun ideas!

● Make a Forever Friends bulletin board. Tape to the center of the display a piece of construction paper with God's name written on it, then tape the character balloons from the story around the bulletin board. Invite children to make balloons of themselves to add to the display, then attach a twisted crepe-paper border. What a colorful reminder that God gives us good friends!

● Have kids brainstorm ways Jesus is our most wonderful friend. Read Matthew 14:27; 18:20; and Luke 18:15-17 and tell how these verses demonstrate that Jesus is our loving and loyal friend. Challenge children to list ways we can show Jesus that we're his friends too.

David and the Giant

1 Samuel 17; 1 Samuel 16:7

What You'll Teach

God knows us by our hearts.

What You'll Need

- For **Say It!** you'll need a Bible, a yardstick, a broom, a sheet of poster board, a paper plate, clear packing tape, markers, scissors, and a brown paper grocery sack.
- For **Play It!** you'll need paper cups, rubber bands, and newspaper.
- For **Pray It!** you'll need an apple cut in half crosswise and a plastic knife. The cut apple should have a crosscut view so that the inside seeds and core resemble a star.

Kid-Clue

You'll be using cool puppets of David and Goliath to tell the story. Practice the story several times to be a super storyteller!

SAY IT!

Before the lesson, you'll need to make David and Goliath stick puppets. Draw David's face on a paper plate, then tape the plate to the top of a yardstick. Round the corners of a sheet of poster board to make a huge head, then draw Goliath's mean face. (See the illustration.) Tape Goliath's head to the bristled portion of the broom. Crumple the paper grocery sack into a pretend stone.

Place the puppets on the floor and hand one child the paper stone. Ask two or three children to stand, then invite the rest of the class to describe what they see when they look at those people.

Say: **When we look at people, we usually see their outside appearances. We might notice how tall they are or the color of their hair or eyes. But God looks at us in a completely different way. Today we'll hear the story of David and Goliath and learn that when God sees us, he sees inside our hearts. You can all help tell the story. When you hear the words *Goliath* or *giant,* stand tall on your tiptoes. And when you hear the name *David,* squat low.**

David and the Giant

Once there were mean soldiers called Philistines. They didn't love God, and they never obeyed him. They were mean and nasty—grrr! But one Philistine was meaner than all the rest— and bigger than all the rest too. His name was *Goliath,* and he was over 9 feet tall! Hold up the big puppet. ***Goliath* would meet God's soldiers on the fighting field every day to laugh at and make fun of God. The Philistines wanted God's soldiers to choose someone to fight *Goliath,* but none of God's soldiers wanted to fight the *giant*— no one, that is, except young *David.*** Hold the small puppet beside the huge one. **But, oh my! *Goliath* was so big, and *David* was so small!**

David* may have been small, but he had a *giant* love for God! When God looked at *David,* he didn't see his small size. God saw the *giant* love and faith in *David's* heart! But *Goliath* just laughed at *David. Hold the big puppet as high as you can. **"You can't hurt me. You're no bigger than a flea!" scoffed *Goliath.***

Wiggle the David puppet as you say: **But *David* chose five smooth stones from the ground and put one stone in his sling. As *Goliath* came toward *David,* he swung the sling and—zzzzing, pop—the *giant* fell with a *giant* plop!** Have the child with the paper stone hurl it at the big puppet, then let the puppet topple over. Hold the David puppet in the air and say: **Yeah, *David!* You might have been young, you might have been small—but your *giant* faith helped *Goliath* to fall!**

Set aside the puppets and read aloud 1 Samuel 16:7. Then ask:

● **How did Goliath see David? How did David see Goliath?** *(Goliath saw David as a weakling; David saw Goliath as big, but not bigger than God!)*

● **What does the Bible mean when it says, "God sees our hearts"?** *(God looks at how we are on the inside—not what we look like on the outside.)*

Say: **I'm so glad that God sees what we're like on the inside, not just on the outside. God really knows who we are because he knows us by our hearts. And there's no fooling God. Goliath found that out! Let's play a game to remind us how God helped David defeat the mean giant.**

PLAY IT!

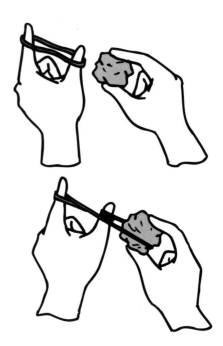

Place six paper cups in the center of the room and invite children to kneel in a circle around the cups. Be sure children are at least 3 feet from the cups. Hand each child a sheet of newspaper and a rubber band. Instruct children to crumple the newspapers into paper stones. Explain that in this game, the cups are giants and the object of the game is to topple the giants by shooting the paper stones from their rubber-band slings. Demonstrate how to stretch a rubber band between your thumb and forefinger, then place the paper wad on the rubber band. Pull back the rubber band and paper wad, then release the paper so it sails through the air!

Each time a cup is toppled, have children shout, "Yeah for God!" Play until all the giants have been toppled. After several games, challenge kids to shoot their paper stones into the trash. Then set aside the rubber bands. Say: **Even though David was small and it seemed impossible to defeat Goliath, God knew better. God knew that David had big faith, and God used that faith to help David defeat the mean giant. Now let's end with a giant prayer thanking God for seeing us on the inside and not just on the outside.**

PRAY IT!

Hold the apple halves together and say: **What do we see when we look at an apple? We see a round fruit with red skin and maybe a stem and leaf. But what do we see on the inside?** Hold apart the apple halves so children can see the insides. Say: **When we look at the inside of an apple, there's a wonderful surprise—a star shape! God looks at the inside of our hearts and sees wonderful things too. He sees our love and the kindness we feel for others. Let's say a prayer thanking God for the way he sees us.** Pray: **Dear God, we're glad you look past our outward appearances. We're thankful you know who we are on the inside. Please help us also try to look at people's hearts and not just their outside appearances. Amen.**

Use the plastic knife to slice the apple, then give everyone a small taste. Remind children that it's what is on the inside that counts!

REPLAY IT!

Try this cool idea to reinforce and enrich today's lesson!

● Let kids make life-size pictures of themselves by lying on white shelf paper and having friends trace around them. Have children draw large heart shapes inside their outlines, then write words that tell about who they are inside their hearts. Words might include honest, faithful, careful, happy, and loving God. Finish by decorating and adding facial features to the outlines. Hang the pictures in a hallway for everyone to enjoy.

Jonah's Stoplight

Jonah 1:1–2:9; Acts 3:19

What You'll Teach

God forgives us when we repent and change.

What You'll Need

- For **Say It!** you'll need a Bible, scissors, black yarn or cord, tape, a sheet of black poster board, and both beads and construction paper in the following colors: red, yellow, and green.
- For **Play It!** you'll need no extra supplies.
- For **Pray It!** you'll need no extra supplies.

Kid-Clue

You'll be stringing stoplight bracelets as you tell the story of Jonah. Practice the story several times to be a super storyteller!

SAY IT!

Before class, cut a 10-inch length of black yarn or cord for each child and one for yourself. Make sure you have several of each color bead for everyone in class. Cut out one red, one green, and one yellow construction-paper circle. You'll use the black poster board as the back of the stoplight.

Set the beads, yarn, paper circles, poster board, and tape beside you. Have kids sit in a circle. Ask them to tell about times they were forgiven or said "I'm sorry." Encourage them to tell how it felt to apologize. Then say: **We all do and say things for which we need God's forgiveness. And God is willing to forgive us if we do three important things. In today's Bible story, Jonah learned what those three** things are. **Let's hear the story of Jonah as we make stoplight bracelets to remind us of God's forgiveness. As you listen, try to discover what those three important forgiveness factors are.** Tell the following story as you assemble the stoplight and lead children in adding beads to their bracelets.

Jonah's Stoplight

God spoke to Jonah. God told Jonah to go to the city of Nineveh and warn the people there that they were doing evil things. But did Jonah obey God? Oh no—Jonah ran! Jonah was afraid to go to Nineveh, so he ran and hid in a dark place on a boat. Tape the black poster board to the wall and hand everyone a black piece of yarn or cord. **Jonah tried to hide from God, but God always knows where we are. The boat set sail, but during the night God sent a terrible storm. The sailors were very afraid, and so was Jonah. But Jonah knew he had caused this trouble, so he told the sailors to toss him overboard. Plop, kersplash! Into the water went Jonah. And as he sank down into the sea, a huge fish swallowed him up!**

There was Jonah, alone in the belly of a fish, alone and frightened. Jonah stopped. Add the red circle to the top of the poster board, then have everyone string a red bead on the yarn. **Jonah knew he had done something very wrong. Jonah knew he had disobeyed God, and he was sorry. Jonah repented, then prayed to God.** Add the yellow circle to the center of the poster board. Have everyone add a yellow bead to the yarn. **Jonah prayed for three days and three nights. And even though Jonah thought he was alone, God was with him. God heard Jonah's prayers for forgiveness, and God answered!**

God forgave Jonah and made the fish spit Jonah out on the sand. Then Jonah jumped up and ran to Nineveh to obey God! Go, Jonah, go! Add the green circle to the bottom of the stoplight and have everyone add a green bead to the bracelet. **Jonah had**

learned that when we need forgiveness we first STOP and admit our mistake. Point to the red light. **Then we YIELD to God and ask his forgiveness.** Point to the yellow light. **And finally, we GO and obey God!** Point to the green light.

Invite children to string additional beads on their bracelets, alternating red, yellow, and green beads. When the bracelets are finished, have children help each other tie the bracelets around their wrists. Then ask:

- **How did Jonah ask for God's forgiveness?**
- **What did Jonah do after God forgave him?**
- **What do we need to do besides say "I'm sorry" to God?**
- **How does God's forgiveness show his love for us?**

Read aloud Jonah 2:9 and Acts 3:19, then say: **We can think of forgiveness as a stoplight. The red light means stop and repent—or admit we're wrong. Yellow means yield to God and ask his forgiveness. And green means go and obey God from now on. When we repent, we're truly sorry for what we've done. And when we change, we don't go back and do those wrong things again. Your bracelet will help you remember the forgiveness stoplight and the three important parts of forgiveness: stop and repent, yield to God through prayer, then go and obey. Now let's play a game to remind us all that God forgives us when we repent and change.**

PLAY IT!

Gently untape the three colored circles from the stoplight. Tape the red circle on one wall, the yellow circle on another wall, and the green circle on a third wall. Have kids stand by the wall without a circle on it. Explain that in this game you'll read a situation in which someone has done something wrong. Have children hop first to the red circle and tell what was done wrong. Then have kids hop to the yellow circle and give a sample sentence asking for God's forgiveness. Finally, have everyone hop to the green circle and tell how to make the situation better or to change the behavior. Use the following situations in the game:

- A toy was stolen from a friend.
- Someone cheated on a test.
- Bad language was used.
- Someone slapped a neighbor.

44

- A lie was told.
- People gossiped about their friends.

When you're through playing, say: **There are many times when we forget and say or do wrong things. We all need God's forgiveness. When we stop and repent, yield to God, then go and obey, God forgives us. And God's forgiveness feels so good! Let's end with a prayer thanking God for his loving forgiveness.**

PRAY IT!

Invite children to find a quiet place to sit. Challenge them to think about one thing they could ask God's forgiveness for today. Then have them touch each bead as you pray the following prayer. **Dear God, we thank you for your gift of forgiveness. We've all done and said things for which we need your forgiveness. As we touch our red beads, we stop and admit we need forgiveness for** (silently fill in the blank). **As we touch the yellow beads, we ask that you forgive us, Lord. And as we touch the green beads, please help us go and obey you as we change our ways. We love you, God. Amen.**

Encourage kids to wear their bracelets until they remember what each color in the forgiveness stoplight means. Remind children that God forgives us when we repent and change.

REPLAY IT!

For lesson reinforcement and enrichment, try this cooperative idea!

- Invite children to turn a door into a giant stoplight. Cover the door with black paper, then have one group of children cut out a huge red circle and label it "Stop and repent!" Have another group cut out a large yellow circle and label it "Yield to God through prayer!" And have a third group cut out a big green circle and label it "Go and obey God!" Tape the circles on the door, then use white chalk to add the title "Forgiveness Stoplight" at the top of the display.

Josiah's Treasure

2 Kings 22; Deuteronomy 11:1

What You'll Teach

God gave us his Word.

What You'll Need

- For **Say It!** you'll need a roll of white shelf paper, a white crayon, watercolor paints, a rubber band, large paintbrushes, newspapers, and scissors.
- For **Play It!** you'll need red and blue ribbon, a marker, rubber bands, plain white paper, and scissors.
- For **Pray It!** you'll need pencils and 6-inch squares of waxed paper.

Kid-Clue

You'll be using a story scroll and paints to tell the story of Josiah finding the Bible. Practice telling the story to be a super storyteller!

SAY IT!

Before class, make a story scroll by cutting a 5-foot length of white shelf paper. Use a white crayon to draw these pictures from left to right across the paper. On the very left of the paper, draw a large picture of a king. (This is Josiah.) Next, draw a big cobweb and spider. Then draw a big mouse, a large leaf, a broken vase, and a scroll. Write the words "Obey God's Word" on the far right side of the paper. You may wish to put a tiny colored dot beside the picture of the king so you remember where to start painting during the story. Roll the paper into a giant scroll and fasten it with a rubber band. Mix several jars of watercolor paint by putting food coloring in water or thinning tempera paints until they're the consistency of watercolor paint. You'll be painting over the white crayon to reveal the hidden pictures during the story.

Place newspapers on the floor and set the paints and paintbrushes around the edge. Gather kids around the newspaper and ask them to tell about times they found something exciting enough to share with others. Then hold up the scroll and say: **In our Bible story today, a young king found an exciting surprise that he wanted to share with others. Let's use this scroll and these paints to tell the story of Josiah and to discover a few of our own hidden surprises.**

Josiah's Treasure

Josiah was a young king who wanted to honor God by cleaning the temple. Paint over the picture of Josiah to reveal the king. **The temple had fallen into great ruin because God's people had neglected it for years. So Josiah sent workmen to repair and clean the temple. What do you think the workmen found as they cleaned? Let's see!** Hand the paintbrush to a child and invite her to paint an area of the story scroll. (But don't reveal the picture of the scroll or the words just yet!) Continue having other children paint until you've revealed all the pictures except the scroll. Then finish telling the rest of the story on the following page.

Say: **Then the workers found the most exciting thing of all.** Paint over the picture of the scroll. **They found a scroll! They ran back to King Josiah, and Josiah had the scroll read. Guess what it was! The scroll contained God's Word—it was part of the Bible! Josiah heard God's words and knew that God's people had not been obeying God. So Josiah changed all that! Josiah called God's people together and read them God's Word.** Paint over the words on the right of the paper. **Josiah read God's Word so all the people could obey God from then on! Yeah, Josiah!**

Set aside the paints, then ask:

● **How was cleaning the temple a way to show love for God?**
● **How is obeying God's Word another way to show our love?**
● **Why was it good that Josiah shared God's Word with others?**
● **How can we thank God for giving us the Bible?**

Say: **Did you know that the Bible is the best-selling book in the history of the world? I'm so glad that Josiah found God's Word, aren't you? Let's play a game to discover what God's Word said to Josiah in that special scroll.**

PLAY IT!

Before the lesson, write "Love the Lord your God and keep … his commands always. Deuteronomy 11:1" on a sheet of paper. Photocopy one verse for each child in class, then roll the papers into scrolls and secure them with rubber bands. Tie red ribbons around half of the scrolls and blue ribbons around the other half. Hide the scrolls around the room.

Form two teams, the Red Team and the Blue Team. Explain that there are scrolls hidden around the room. When you say "go," kids are to search for a scroll that matches the color of their team. When a scroll is found, the player must exchange it with someone from the other color team. For example, when a player on the Red Team finds a scroll with a red ribbon, he must hand the scroll to someone on the Blue Team.

When kids all have scrolls that are different from their team colors, have them open the scrolls and read them aloud. Then briefly discuss why Josiah shared God's Word with the Israelites and why God wants us to share his Word today. Then say: **God gave us his Word so we could learn more about him and how to obey him. And just as God shared his Word with us, we can share God's Word with others. Let's end with a prayer thanking God for the Bible. We'll use our Scripture papers to help us.**

PRAY IT!

Hand each child a pencil and a piece of waxed paper. Have children place the waxed paper on their Scripture scrolls from *Play It!*—waxy side down. Remind children that Josiah found a great treasure when he found God's Word. Then challenge each child to write a word that describes a treasure found in God's Word, such as truth, love, learning, and faith. Press firmly on the waxed paper to write the word or words, then remove the waxed paper. Invite children to exchange their papers and gently use the sides of the pencil lead to color over the hidden words and reveal what they say.

Collect all the papers, then end with a prayer thanking God for his wonderful gift. Pray: **Dear God, thank you for sharing your Word with us in the Bible. We thank you for the** (read the words from the papers) **that you give us through your Word. Please help us read the Bible every day to learn more about you and your Word. Amen.**

Remind children that God gave us his Word to read and to share with others. Have kids put the Scripture scrolls in their Bibles for safekeeping.

REPLAY IT!

Use this super idea to reinforce and enrich the lesson!

● Children love receiving mail! Hand each child a piece of paper, a postage stamp, and an envelope. Write favorite Scripture verses on the papers, then decorate the papers and envelopes. Give each child the name and address of another child in class to secretly send their Scripture notes to. Be sure everyone will receive a special delivery. Then mail the envelopes and see how sharing God's Word makes everyone smile!

The Furnace of Fire

Daniel 3; Deuteronomy 5:8-10

What You'll Teach

We worship only one God.

What You'll Need

- For **Say It!** you'll need a Bible, tape, a large ribbon spool or a stiff piece of cardboard, twigs or wooden stakes, and 10 yards each of yellow, red, and orange paper ribbon (available very inexpensively from craft or fabric stores).
- For **Play It!** you'll need scissors, tape, Bingo daubers, markers, and paint-stirring sticks (available free from hardware stores).
- For **Pray It!** you'll need no supplies.

Kid-Clue

You'll be using lots of colorful ribbon to tell the story of the fiery furnace. Practice the story several times to be a super storyteller!

SAY IT!

Before class, tape the ribbons together to form a 30-yard length. Begin with the yellow ribbon, then add the orange, then the red. Wind the ribbon on a spool or around a stiff piece of cardboard. This story is best told outdoors where there's a lot of room to unwind the ribbon!

Gather children at one end of the storytelling area. Hold the spool of ribbon and say: **There are many things we shouldn't do. We shouldn't cross the street without**

Storyteller TIPS

If it's a windy day, place stones or heavy books on the unwound ribbon to keep it in place.

50

looking. **We shouldn't be rude or unkind to other people. And we shouldn't steal things or tell lies. What are some other things we shouldn't do?** Let children tell their ideas, then say: **What if someone told you to do something you knew was wrong. What would you do? Well, that's what happened to three friends in the Bible. Today we'll learn what they did—or rather, what they didn't do! This spool of ribbon will help us tell the story.**

The Furnace of Fire

Long ago, King Nebuchadnezzar (ne-bu-cad-NEZ-ar) **ruled the land of Babylon. The Babylonians didn't know or love God, but King Nebuchadnezzar had three servants who loved God very much. Their names were Shadrach, Meshach, and Abednego. They loved and worshiped only God. One day, King Nebuchadnezzar built a huge golden statue. How huge was it? Let's see!** Hold the end of the ribbon and have kids unwind it to its full length of 90 feet. (You may have to shout for this part!) **The statue was 90 feet tall and 9 feet wide! Now that's a huge statue!** Tie the ends of the ribbon to twigs or wooden stakes and push them into the ground. Then line everyone up at the yellow end and say: **King Nebuchadnezzar ordered everyone in the land to bow down and pray to that big golden idol. What do you think the friends did? What would you do?** Shadrach, Meshach, and Abednego said,

> *No way, no how! We'll never get on our knees to bow!*
> *We only worship the God who's true.*
> *We'll never worship the likes of you!*

Take six giant steps if you agree with these three friends. Pause for kids to take their steps. Continue: **King Nebuchadnezzar was very angry! He said he would toss them into a furnace of fire if they wouldn't bow down. But what did the friends say?**

> *No way, no how! We'll never get on our knees to bow!*
> *We only worship the God who's true.*

We'll never worship the likes of you!

Take six giant steps if you agree. Pause, then say: **The king turned up the heat in the furnace. Yow! Take six hot-hops—but do not bow! Then the king tossed the three friends into the furnace—whoosh! But these friends kept saying,**

No way, no how! We'll never get on our knees to bow!
We only worship the God who's true.
We'll never worship the likes of you!

Take six giant steps if you agree. Pause, then say: **Shadrach, Meshach, and Abednego chose to die rather than to worship a false idol. But did they die? No siree! Take six more hops to show your glee!** Pause, then continue: **God sent an angel to save them! The friends and the angel walked around in the furnace, and when the friends came out, they were unhurt! King Nebuchadnezzar was amazed and knew how powerful God was. The king told the friends they could worship God from then on. And what did the friends say?**

We love you, God, and that is true.
Nothing can keep us from worshiping you!

Now hop to the end of the ribbon and then shout, "We love you, God," to worship him!

Pause until everyone reaches the end of the ribbon, then discuss why it was wise and brave of the three friends to worship only God. Read aloud Deuteronomy 5:8-10. Then say: **God tells us to worship only him. And that's just what Shadrach, Meshach, and Abednego did! We can worship God too. Let's use our fiery ribbons in this worship craft activity.**

PLAY IT!

Distribute the sticks used for stirring paint. Invite kids to decorate the sticks with the Bingo daubers and markers. Let each child cut a 3-foot section of ribbon to tape to one end of her stick. If there's enough ribbon, let each child attach two or three ribbon streamers. Finally, help children write "Worship God!" on their sticks.

When the worship streamers are complete, form two groups and teach kids the following worship cheer. After groups are familiar with their parts, shake the streamers and worship God with the worship cheer several times. Then switch sides and cheer again!

SIDE ONE	SIDE TWO
Who do you worship?	We only worship God!
Who do you pray to?	We only pray to God!
Who do you praise?	We only praise our God!
Who do you honor?	We only honor God!
Who do you love?	We love God!

After everyone has had a turn to repeat both sides of the worship cheer, say: **Worshiping God can be such fun. And there are lots of ways to worship God. We can worship God through cheering, singing, reading the Bible, and being kind to others. We can also worship God through prayer. Let's worship God with a quiet prayer asking God to help us worship him every day.**

PRAY IT!

Have children form a circle and hold the worship sticks of the people beside them. Pray: **Dear God, we're so glad we can worship you. We worship you because you are loving and powerful. We worship you because you are the only God. And we worship you because we love you. Please help us find new ways to worship you every day. Amen.** Have children repeat the worship cheer one more time, then shake their streamers with joy.

REPLAY IT!

Reinforce and enrich your lesson with this fun idea!

● Make Fiery Furnace candles to remind you to worship God every day. Have children use small straight pins and tiny beads to decorate the lower half and base of chunky white candles. Poke the pins through the tiny beads, then poke the pins into the lower halves of the candles. Have children place the candles on their dining tables at home, and encourage them to ask adults to light the candles at mealtime as their families worship God with prayers of thanksgiving.

That's No "Lion"!

Daniel 6; Psalm 91:15

What You'll Teach

God hears our prayers.

What You'll Need

- For **Say It!** you'll need a Bible, two paper grocery sacks, glue, markers, scissors, and photocopies of the lion and Daniel from the story box on page 55. Make one copy of Daniel and three copies of the lion.
- For **Play It!** you'll need newspapers.
- For **Pray It!** you'll need lunch sacks, markers, crayons, glitter glue, scissors, glue, and one photocopy of the lion pattern on page 55 for each child.

Kid-Clue

You'll be using a tricky paper bag to tell the story of Daniel in the lions' den. Practice several times to be a super storyteller!

SAY IT!

Before class prepare the special storytelling bag by cutting the side from one of the paper bags. Glue three edges of the cut side to the side of the whole paper bag, but leave a space along the top edge. This will make a secret pocket.

Photocopy and color the figures from page 55, then cut them out. Prepare one cutout of Daniel and three of the lion.

Gather kids and set the paper bag lions' den and the cutouts beside you. Ask children to tell how God has answered their prayers. Then say:

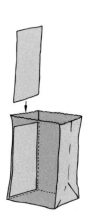

Our Bible story is about a time God heard and answered prayer, and it's an especially exciting story! You can help tell the story. Each time you hear the word *Daniel,* kneel and hold your hands as if in prayer. Each time you hear me say the word *king,* shake your finger and look grouchy. And every time you hear me say the word *lion* or *lions,* make snarly growls.

That's No "Lion"!

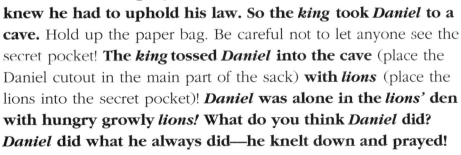

Hold up the figure of Daniel and say: **This is *Daniel. Daniel* loved God, and he also loved praying to God. Three times a day *Daniel* would kneel and give thanks for all God had done for him. *Daniel* would also ask for God's guidance and help. Now *Daniel* lived in Babylon, where *King* Darius (DARE-ee-us) ruled the land. The *king* didn't love God, but he did like *Daniel.* He thought *Daniel* was wise. Then one day *King* Darius made a new law. The *king* decreed that everyone should pray to him—not to any other man or thing, not even to God. What do you think *Daniel* did when he heard about the law? *Daniel* did what he always did—he knelt down and prayed!**

When *King* Darius heard about *Daniel* and his prayers, he knew he had to uphold his law. So the *king* took *Daniel* to a cave. Hold up the paper bag. Be careful not to let anyone see the secret pocket! **The *king* tossed *Daniel* into the cave** (place the Daniel cutout in the main part of the sack) **with *lions*** (place the lions into the secret pocket)! ***Daniel* was alone in the *lions'* den with hungry growly *lions*! What do you think *Daniel* did? *Daniel* did what he always did—he knelt down and prayed!**

All night long, *Daniel* stayed in the *lions'* den. *King* Darius thought *Daniel* would surely be eaten. What do you think the *king* saw when he went to the *lions'* den the next morning? Hold the secret pocket shut to keep the lion cutouts from falling out, then turn the sack upside down so the figure of Daniel tumbles out. **The *king* saw *Daniel* unharmed! *Daniel* explained how he had prayed and how God had sent an angel to close the mouths of the *lions*. God had saved *Daniel!* Then *King* Darius made a new law that told everyone to fear and respect God, for he powerfully saved *Daniel* from the *lions*. Now *Daniel* could pray whenever he wanted! So remember what *Daniel* learned:**

Just keep prayin'—just keep tryin', *(Make prayer motions.)*
And God will help you—that's no lyin'! *(Growl.)*

Set the paper bag and figures aside, then ask:

● **Why is it important to pray to God?**

● **Why do you think God answers our prayers?**

● **Does God always give you the answers you want? Explain.**

Say: **Let's learn more about praying by reading from the Bible.** Read aloud Psalm 91:15, then say: **Daniel learned that God really does hear and answer our prayers. God may not always give us the answer we want or answer when we think he should, but we can trust God to hear and answer in his time and in his way. Let's play a fun game to remind us that we can pray to God no matter what!**

PLAY IT!

Wad three newspapers into paper balls. Form two groups and name one group the Daniels and the other the lions. Have the lions form a large circle around the group of Daniels. Instruct the Daniels to choose three team members to be angels who stand outside the circle. Explain that angels will try to free the Daniels from the lions' den by tossing paper balls to them. If a Daniel catches a ball, he is free and becomes an angel to help free other team members. The lions can block, deflect, or toss the paper balls away from the angels. Play continues for 3 minutes or until all the Daniels have been freed. Then switch roles and have the lions become the Daniels.

When the game is over, discuss how God answered Daniel's prayer by sending an angel to close the lions' mouths. Invite children to tell how God has answered their prayers. Then say: **God loves us so much that he wants to hear our prayers. And because God is mighty and full of love, he answers our prayers. Just as Daniel gave his troubles to God, we can approach God with our worries and problems. Let's make prayer sacks to help give our troubles to God and his loving power.**

PRAY IT!

Hand each child a paper lion and two paper lunch sacks. Demonstrate how to cut the side from one of the bags and glue it in place to make a secret pocket. Prepare the sacks just as you prepared the storytelling bag. Then invite kids to use markers, crayons, and glitter glue to decorate their prayer bags and lions.

When the prayer bags are complete, have children think of one worry or problem they could pray for right now and write their prayer requests on the backs of the lions. Then have children follow along as you pray: **Dear God, we thank you for loving us enough to hear and to answer our prayers. Sometimes our troubles and worries are like lions waiting to gobble us up. We want to give you those lions right now, God. Please help us with** (have children think of their prayer requests as they slide the paper lions into the secret pockets). **Thank you, God, for your incredible help, your amazing power, and your awesome love. In Jesus' name, amen.** Encourage children to write their prayer requests on slips of paper each day and drop them in their prayer sacks to remind them to give their worries to God.

REPLAY IT!

Try one of these fun ideas for lesson reinforcement and enrichment!

● Use the figure of Daniel and the lion cutouts to make Bible-story mobiles. Simply photocopy the figures onto stiff paper, then cut them out. (You can make a whole denful of lions!) Color the figures, then use fishing line to suspend them from clothes hangers or drinking straws. Add index cards with Psalm 91:15 written on them.

● Use the lion cutouts and a shoe-box lions' den to play a Scripture-memory game. Form two teams and hand each team ten lions to color as their team lions. Each time a team correctly repeats a Scripture verse, add a team lion to the den. See how many lions a team can collect in a Scripture-memory game or during the next month of reviews!

The Gift of Love

Luke 2:1-7; John 3:16

What You'll Teach

Jesus is God's gift of love.

What You'll Need

- For **Say It!** you'll need scissors, a pencil, red markers, and one photocopy of the box pattern from page 110. Use stiff paper such as card stock for the photocopy.
- For **Play It!** you'll need a Bible.
- For **Pray It!** you'll need paper and markers.

Kid-Clue

You'll be folding a special box to tell the Christmas story. Practice folding and unfolding the box several times to be a super storyteller!

SAY IT!

Before class, photocopy on stiff paper the box pattern (solid and dotted lines) from page 110. You may need an adult to help with this. Cut along the solid lines, then cut out slots A and B. Fold and crease the dotted lines upward. Use a red marker to color the hearts on the sides of the box without lines. Use the directions below and the illustrations on the next page to practice folding the box.

Step 1: Pinch the folded hearts together and carefully bring the sides of the box upward.

Storyteller TIPS

• Fold the box several times before the story to make folding it easier. Be sure to fold exactly on the dotted lines!

• Young children especially enjoy this story. Consider having your class present the story to a younger class and help them fold their own story boxes.

Step 2: Tuck in the side flaps, then slip slots A and B over the folded hearts. Push the slots down as far as they'll go.

Step 3: Open the hearts to secure the completed box.

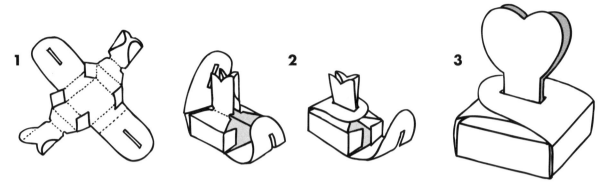

Seat listeners in a circle on the floor. Place the unfolded box beside you. Ask children to tell about special gifts they've received and why they were special. Then say: **Gifts are loved for many different reasons. But there is one gift that is more wonderful than all the others combined! Let's hear a story about the most perfect gift in the world and how that gift keeps giving love to everyone who receives it.**

The Gift of Love

Hold the hearts on the ends of the box and say: **Mary and Joseph knew they were chosen to bring God's wonderful gift into the world. They were very excited when God told them about his gift. God had also told them to travel to the town of Bethlehem, where his wonderful gift would be given to the world. So Mary and Joseph folded blankets** (fold the sides of the hearts and pinch them together) **and laid them on the back of their donkey. Then Mary climbed on the donkey and away they went—trip, trot, trip, trot** (hold the sides of the box on the floor and gently push the hearts up and down to mimic a donkey ride), **clip, clop, clop. As they walked along, Mary and Joseph thought about God's perfect gift and how God's gift would bring love into the world.**

They finally reached Bethlehem, but where would they stay? Where would God's gift be brought into the world? Joseph saw an inn and knocked on the door—tap, tap, tap. Knock on the

59

floor. **But the innkeeper answered, "There's no room here!" and closed the door, whump!** Fold one end of the box up and slide the slot over the folded hearts. **Poor Mary and Joseph. No room here, no room there, no place or space anywhere! But wait—what did Joseph see?** Hold the open end of the box so kids can peek inside. **Joseph saw a small cave being used as a stable! It was cozy and warm and full of animals. What animal sounds did they hear?** Encourage children to make the appropriate animal sounds with you. **Cows and horses, birds and sheep; even a field mouse, fast asleep!** Close the open end of the box and slide the slot over the folded hearts. **In that cozy place, God brought his glorious gift into the world! What was God's gift?** Unfold the hearts and show them to the children. **God's gift was Jesus and the love he brings us! And God's gift is for everyone who chooses to love and follow Jesus. Isn't that a perfect gift of love?**

Set the box down and ask:
- **How did God show his love in giving us Jesus?**
- **Why is Jesus the perfect gift?**
- **How can this gift of love spread to others?**

Say: **God gave us a perfect gift of love when he gave us Jesus. And through Jesus' love, the gift keeps growing! We can help spread the gift of Jesus' love to others too. Let's play a game and learn about spreading the gift of love to others.**

PLAY IT!

Choose one child to be the tagger. Explain that this game is played much like chain tag. When the tagger tags someone he tells something about Jesus' love such as "Jesus' love is for everyone" or "Jesus' love is perfect love." The tagged player then links elbows with the tagger and may help tag and tell others about Jesus' love. Continue cooperatively tagging and telling others about Jesus' love until everyone is joined in a long line. Then form a circle and ask:

● **What are things we can tell others about Jesus' love?**

● **How is telling others about Jesus like giving them a wonderful gift?**

Read aloud John 3:16, then say: **Jesus is the gift that keeps giving—giving us love, forgiveness, help, faith, and even eternal life. When we tell others about Jesus and his perfect love, it's like giving them the best gift of love in the world! Let's end with a prayer thanking God for Jesus and his love.**

PRAY IT!

Have children get into pairs. If an older class is presenting this activity to a younger class, pair the younger children with older kids. Hand each child a piece of paper and a marker. Briefly discuss things that are true about Jesus' love, such as Jesus' love is forgiving, Jesus' love helps us be kind, Jesus' love heals broken hearts, and Jesus' love helps us love others. Have children write "Jesus' love" sentences on their papers. Encourage the older children to write what their younger partners dictate.

Form a prayer circle and have children hold their slips of paper. Tell kids that you'll offer a prayer thanking God for his gift of love through Jesus but that when you pause, they are to take turns reading or telling what is on their papers. Pray: **Dear God, we thank you for your gift of perfect love through Jesus. We know that Jesus is the gift that keeps giving us more love. Jesus' love is** (pause for kids to read their papers one at a time). **Please help us find ways to spread the gift of Jesus' love to others. Amen.**

End by encouraging children to decorate their papers, then slip the papers inside the gift box used to tell the Bible story. Decorate the sides of the box, then present the gift to someone in your church or community who might need a reminder of Jesus' love.

REPLAY IT!

To reinforce and enrich today's lesson, try this festive idea!

● Have kids make their own special gift boxes! Photocopy and enlarge the pattern on page 110 onto red or green construction paper, one for each child. Have an adult cut the slits. Show kids how to cut out and fold the boxes, then decorate the projects with ribbon, glitter glue, markers, or holiday stickers. Fill the gift boxes with red and green wrapped candies and small Scripture cards with John 3:16 written on them.

Follow Me!

Mark 3:13-19; Matthew 4:19, 20

What You'll Teach

We can choose to follow Jesus.

What You'll Need

- For **Say It!** you'll need a Bible, scissors, markers, tape, balloons, and a photocopy of the disciple ID cards from page 111.
- For **Play It!** you'll need the disciple ID cards from *Say It!*
- For **Pray It!** you'll need markers, index cards, and scissors.

Kid-Clue

You'll use balloons and special ID cards to tell how Jesus chose the first disciples. Practice several times to be a super storyteller!

SAY IT!

Before the lesson, photocopy a set of the disciple ID cards from page 111. Color the cards and cut them out. Inflate twelve balloons and tape one ID card to the knot on each balloon. Finally, draw a different face on each of the balloons.

Set the balloons beside you and gather children in a circle. Ask them to tell about ways they choose their friends and why careful choices are important. Then say: **Jesus chose his friends and followers wisely too. Our Bible story today is about the time Jesus chose his first**

Storyteller TIPS

If kids get a bit noisy passing or bopping the balloons during the story, have them sit in a circle and calmly pass the balloons instead!

62

twelve followers, who were called disciples. Let's stand in a circle so you can meet the disciples Jesus chose! Place the balloons on the floor in the center of the circle, then tell the following story.

Follow Me!

Jesus was walking by the Sea of Galilee when he spotted two fishermen. The men were brothers, and their names were Simon and Andrew. Jesus said to them, "Come, follow me, and I will make you fishers of men." At once, Simon and Andrew left their fishing nets to follow Jesus. Let's find out more about Simon and Andrew. Have two kids fish through the balloons to find Simon and Andrew, then read the ID cards aloud to learn more about the brothers. Have children begin to pass the balloons around the circle as you continue the story.

Jesus had chosen two followers, but soon he chose more. Once again Jesus chose two brothers, but these brothers' names were James and John. The brothers were in a boat with their father and others. They were all fishing until Jesus called James and John to follow him. And what did they do? James and John followed! Invite two more kids to find the balloons labeled James and John, then read the ID cards aloud. Pass these balloons in addition to the first two and continue the story. **Jesus had chosen his first four followers, whose names were Simon, Andrew, James, and John. Then Jesus walked by a lake and called Levi, who later changed his name to Matthew. Matthew followed Jesus right away!** Have one child find the Matthew balloon and read the ID card aloud. Pass the Matthew balloon with the others.

Jesus had chosen five followers, but soon he chose seven more! Have seven children choose the rest of the balloons and read each ID card aloud, then gently pass all twelve balloons around the circle.

Say: **Let's see who Jesus chose. Stop the balloons!** Have children holding balloons read the names of the disciples.

Then end with this rhyme:

To Simon, Andrew, James, and John,
Jesus called and said, "Come on!"
Matthew, Philip, Thomas too.
Then he chose Bartholomew.
Another Simon, another James—
Can you remember all their names?
Then Jesus chose Thaddaeus
and the betrayer named Judas.
Twelve disciples, that is true—
But we can be his followers too!

Set aside the balloons, then ask:

- **How do you think the disciples felt when Jesus called them?**
- **What were the disciples called to do?**
- **What did Jesus mean when he said, "I'll make you fishers of men"?**
- **How can we be Jesus' followers today?**

Read aloud Mark 3:13-19. Then say: **Jesus chose special people to be his followers. And when we know and love Jesus, we can be his special followers too! We can tell others about Jesus' love and forgiveness. We can spread kindness to others. And we can pray and read the Bible to learn more about Jesus. Let's play a game to help us learn the names of Jesus' first twelve followers.**

PLAY IT!

Gently untape the disciple ID cards from the balloons and place them in a row on the floor in the center of the room. Form two teams and have them stand on opposite sides and about 3 feet away from the cards. If you have more than twenty-four children, form three or four teams. Have each team number off so there's at least one pair of children with each number. Explain that in this lively game, a disciple's name and a number will be called. The two children with that number race to snatch the disciple's ID card and return to their place in line. If the child who snatched the card is tagged by the other player before reaching her place in line, the other player gets to keep the card. If the child snatching the card makes it back to her place without being tagged, her team keeps the card. To avoid collisions, tell children they must hop, not run! Play until all the disciple cards have been snatched. The team with the most cards wins and may line up first for drinks of water.

End by challenging volunteers to name all twelve disciples. Then say: **The disciples wanted to follow and serve Jesus. I'm so glad that Jesus wants us to be his disciples too. It's a special honor and privilege to serve Jesus. Let's end with a prayer asking Jesus to help us become good followers.**

PRAY IT!

Before class, cut index cards in half so you have one half card for each child. Invite children to sit in a circle and hand everyone a card. Set the markers in the center of the circle. Read aloud Matthew 4:19, 20, then say: **When we know and love Jesus, we can be his followers. What are ways we can follow and serve Jesus?** Encourage children to review ways to serve Jesus, such as telling others about Jesus' love and forgiveness, being kind to others, and praying. Then invite children to write on their cards one way they can follow Jesus during the coming week and sign their names on their Disciple Cards as a sign of their desire to follow and serve Jesus. If you have time, encourage children to decorate their Disciple Cards.

> I will help my brother
> with his homework.
> JENNIFER

End with this prayer: **Dear Lord, we're so glad that you chose to love us. We want to choose you too. Please help us find ways to follow and serve you as the first disciples did. With our love in Jesus' name, amen.** Encourage children to put their Disciple Cards in their billfolds, Bibles, or pockets as reminders that they can choose to know, love, and follow Jesus every day.

REPLAY IT!

For reinforcement and enrichment, try one of these neat ideas!

● Make a fun matching game kids can take home. Hand each child an envelope and two sets of disciple ID cards to color and cut out. (Photocopy the cards on stiff paper for durability!) Shuffle the cards and turn them face down. Have kids get with partners and take turns turning over the cards to make matches as they name the disciples. Store the cards in the envelopes.

Don't Rock the Boat!

Luke 8:22-25; Luke 12:32

What You'll Teach

Jesus calms our fears.

What You'll Need

- For **Say It!** you'll need a Bible, sturdy folding tables, and small fireplace logs.
- For **Play It!** you'll need no extra supplies.
- For **Pray It!** you'll need no extra supplies.

 ## Kid-Clue

You'll be using a rocking table to tell the story of how Jesus calmed the storm. Practice several times to be a super storyteller!

SAY IT!

Place the table upside down on the floor with the legs folded out. Position the small fireplace log under and in the center of the table. This should create a rocking table for children to sit on. Use a table and log for every four to five children.

Have children sit on the floor around the table (or tables). Ask them to tell about times they were afraid. Encourage kids to share what helped them be brave when they were afraid. Allow time for several responses, then say: **Did you know that on one stormy night, Jesus' disciples were very afraid? Our Bible story today is about**

Storyteller TIPS

If you don't have enough tables and logs, simply have kids sit in a pretend boat on the floor and rock back and forth as they make stormy sound effects.

66

that time and how Jesus calmed their fears in an amazing way. Then tell the following Bible story about Jesus calming the disciples' fears.

Don't Rock the Boat!

It all started out one night when Jesus and the disciples got into a boat. Let's sit in our pretend boat. Have children find places to sit on the table. **Be careful—don't rock the boat! It was a nice night for a sail. The stars were out, and the water was smooth and calm. Jesus was sleepy from teaching all day, so he fell asleep in the boat.**

Suddenly, there was a big clap of thunder—boom! Encourage everyone to sound like thunder. **Crash, boom-boom! Lightning was flashing, thunder was boom-ing, and the wind whistled and blew. Aaaooooo! Blow like the wind!** Begin gently rocking back and forth. **The wind and waves rocked the little boat so hard that the disciples thought they were all going to drown! "Help! We need Jesus! How can he sleep when we might drown?" The disciples ran to wake Jesus.** Continue gently rocking back and forth.

"Jesus! We're going to drown!" Jesus stood by the edge of the boat and said, "Wind, be still! Waves, be still!" And guess what happened then? Slowly stop rocking the tables until they're still. Whisper: **The wind became still, and the waves became calm. The disciples weren't afraid any longer. They weren't afraid, but they were amazed! Then Jesus said, "Where is your faith?" The disciples wondered who this was who could command the wind and the waves to obey him. Who was he? He was Jesus! The disciples learned that night that Jesus can do anything—even calm our fears!**

Carefully climb out of the pretend boats, then ask:

● **Why do you think Jesus calmed the sea that night?**
● **What did Jesus mean when he asked, "Where is your faith?"**
● **How can our faith in Jesus help calm our fears?**

Read aloud Luke 12:32, then say: **Jesus tells us not to be afraid. That's because when we trust Jesus and put our faith in him, Jesus helps us calm our fears. It's like having a perfect lifeboat in the middle of a stormy sea. We can trust Jesus' help. Let's play a lifeboat game to remind us that Jesus can calm our fears.**

PLAY IT!

Have children stand in the center of the room. Explain that in this lively game, they'll be forming lifeboat crews. Explain that you'll call out a number and everyone must rush to form a "lifeboat" with that many people. For example, if you call out the number three, kids must quickly get into groups of three. If you call seven, they must form groups of seven. If there are kids left out of a lifeboat, they can decide what number to call next. For an added challenge, have kids form their lifeboat crews in less than 1 minute!

Play several rounds, then end the game by having children form one large lifeboat crew. Then have kids sit in place and visit about ways to give our fears to Jesus, such as through prayer, through reading the Bible, through the friends Jesus gives us, and through our loving parents. Point out to children that Jesus may send us help in the form of other people and that we may be called to be Jesus' lifeboats too.

Say: **Because Jesus loves us, he wants to help us just as he helped the disciples that stormy night. But just like the disciples, we need to have more faith in Jesus and trust him to care for us. When we trust and put our faith in Jesus, he can calm our fears. Let's end with a prayer thanking Jesus for his help and asking him to strengthen our faith.**

PRAY IT!

Have children sit on the rocking tables again. Take turns naming things that make us afraid. Each time a child tells something that makes him fearful or worried, have everyone gently rock the boat, shout "Jesus helps us!" and then stop rocking. When everyone has had a turn, pray: **Dear Lord, we're glad you love us and want to help us not be afraid or worried. We want our faith in you to keep growing stronger every day. Please help us trust in you when we feel afraid, lonely, or worried. Amen.**

Explain that going through life is like rowing a boat across the sea. When times get rough, Jesus helps us stay afloat! End by singing this song to the tune of "Row, Row, Row Your Boat." Encourage kids to gently rock back and forth in the pretend boat as they sing.

Jesus cares for us
When we row our boats.
There's no fear with Jesus near—
His love keeps us afloat.

REPLAY IT!

Use this cool craft idea to reinforce and enrich the lesson!

● Make boats-in-a-bottle by cutting small boats from sponge. Fill clear plastic soda-pop bottles with water, then add several drops of blue food coloring. Stuff the sponge boats into the bottles, then replace the bottle tops securely. Shake, rattle, and roll the bottles to make stormy seas. Then watch as the waters calm and remember how Jesus calmed the sea—along with the disciples' fears!

The Miracle Dinner

John 6:1-13; Philippians 4:19

What You'll Teach

God provides for us.

What You'll Need

- For **Say It!** you'll need a Bible, scissors, brown poster board, a picnic basket, a small towel, paper flowers, pictures of people cut from magazines or coloring books, and tuna-salad sandwiches in plastic sandwich bags. Prepare 1/4 of a sandwich for each child, plus a few extras.
- For **Play It!** you'll need newspapers, plastic sandwich bags, paper lunch sacks, tape, colored tissue paper, and permanent markers.
- For **Pray It!** you'll need no extra supplies.

Kid-Clue

You'll be using a surprise basket to tell the story of Jesus feeding the five thousand. Practice the story several times to be a super storyteller!

SAY IT!

Before class, make a storytelling basket with a secret panel by cutting a piece of poster board to fit the bottom of the basket. Put the wrapped sandwiches in the bottom of the basket and lay the poster board over them. Place the small towel in the basket so the edges drape over the sides of the basket. Place the paper flowers and the pictures of the people in the basket. Set the Bible beside the basket.

Storyteller TIPS

If you don't have a picnic basket, a laundry basket will work just fine as your storytelling basket!

Gather kids and invite them to tell what kinds of things we need to live, such as shelter, food, water, and air. Then say: **Our Bible story today is about a time when lots of people needed something and about how Jesus miraculously provided it. When you know what the people needed, put one hand on your head. When you know how Jesus provided what they needed, say, "Thank you, Lord!"** Set the picnic basket in front of you and begin.

The Miracle Dinner

One day many years ago, Jesus and his disciples were on a hillside. They were outside, and the day was beautiful. Reach into the basket and pull out the paper flowers. **Many people were with Jesus. In fact, there were five thousand people.** Pull the pictures of the people from the picnic basket. **Now *that's* a crowd! The people had come to listen to and learn from Jesus. And Jesus taught them about God and his love.** Pick up the Bible. **Jesus taught them about obeying God and being kind to each other. Jesus taught the people all day, but when it was late, they began to get very hungry. Their hearts and minds were full of Jesus' teachings—but their tummies were empty!** Tip the picnic basket slightly so everyone can see that it's empty. (Don't tip out the hidden goodies!)

Jesus looked at his disciples and asked, "Where shall we get food to feed these hungry people?" Philip said that eight month's of pay wouldn't buy enough to give each a single bite. Then Andrew saw a little boy with five small loaves of bread and two small fish. But how could so little food feed so many people? Still Jesus said, "Have everyone sit down."

Hold up a tuna sandwich in a plastic bag. **Jesus took the bread and fish and gave thanks for them. Then he fed everyone with that fish and bread!** Hand out the tuna-salad sandwiches, but have children wait before munching them. Continue: **There was plenty to eat, and no one was hungry. There were even leftovers!**

71

Show the extra sandwiches in the basket. **Jesus supplied the hungry people's need through his power in God. And the Lord supplies our needs too!**

Say a prayer thanking God for his provision, then invite children to nibble their sandwiches as you ask:

- **Why do you think Jesus performed a miracle to feed the people?**
- **How did Jesus feeding the five thousand show them his love?**
- **In what ways does the Lord provide for us?**
- **How can we thank God for his loving care?**

Read aloud Philippians 4:19, then say: **Because God loves us, he provides for us. From food to water to his Word in the Bible, God helps us by supplying what we need. Let's play a helping game to remind us of how the Lord provided bread and fish for the five thousand people.**

PLAY IT!

Set the craft materials on the floor in the center of the play area. Have children form pairs, then have partners decide who will make a fish and who will make a loaf of bread. Explain that in this craft activity, children must help by supplying the craft materials that their partners need to finish their craft projects. For example, children making fish will need plastic sandwich bags, colored tissue paper, tape, and markers. Children making loaves of bread will need paper lunch sacks, newspapers, markers, and tape. Children cannot get their own craft materials but must ask their partners to supply them.

To make a fish, stuff colored tissue paper inside a plastic sandwich bag, then wrap tape around the end of the bag, leaving about 1 inch of bag to make the tail. Use permanent markers to add eyes and fins. To make a loaf of bread, stuff a paper lunch sack with newspapers, then fold the end over and tape it securely to the underside of the bag. Draw brown crust lines on top of the bag.

When the crafts are complete, ask children what it was like to rely on someone else to supply their needs. Did anyone remember to say thank-you?

Say: **The Lord knows what we need even before we ask him. And he provides for our needs in many ways—even through using other people. It's important to remember to thank God for all he gives us and all the help he sends, so let's offer a prayer right now with thanksgiving in our hearts.**

PRAY IT!

Place the picnic basket from *Say It!* in the center of the room and gather kids around it holding the craft items they made. Say: **As we pray, let's take turns naming things we're glad God provides for us, such as food, shelter, loving people, and the Bible. As you name something God gives us, place your fish or loaf of bread in the basket.** Pray: **Dear God, we're so thankful for all that you provide for us. We couldn't live without you or your wonderful love. We want to take time right now to thank you for** (name things to be thankful for, then place the craft items in the basket). **With all the good things you give us, the best thing is your love! We love you too. Amen.**

As kids leave, invite them to take their craft projects home. If any projects are left, use them in a bulletin-board display to remind everyone how Jesus miraculously provided food for the five thousand. Use duct tape to attach a laundry basket to the bulletin board, then attach the bread and fish around it, along with the words "My God will supply all your needs."

REPLAY IT!

To reinforce and enrich today's lesson, try one of these fun ideas!

● Suggest that the class hold a soup-stretcher supper to see how many church members they can feed from several large pots of vegetable soup or chili. Be sure to add crispy crackers and fruit to the menu. Have your class retell the story of Jesus feeding the five thousand, then lead everyone in a thank-you prayer to God for all he provides.

● Ask a church leader if anyone in the congregation is in need of help such as yard work, clothing, or money. Then have the class brainstorm ways to provide for that person's needs through their own time, money, talents, donation drives, or other means. Remind children that God often sends us to help provide for other people's needs.

Forgive and Forget

Luke 19:1-10; Matthew 6:14, 15

What You'll Teach

Jesus forgives us.

What You'll Need

- For **Say It!** you'll need a Bible, newspapers, scissors, a rubber band, tape, brown paper, paper coins, and a photocopy of "Daniel" from page 55.
- For **Play It!** you'll need newspapers, scissors, rubber bands, tape, markers, and construction paper.
- For **Pray It!** you'll need no extra supplies.

Kid-Clue

You'll be using a neat newspaper tree to tell the story of Zacchaeus. Practice the story several times to be a super storyteller!

SAY IT!

Before class, prepare a rolled paper tree. Begin by opening up a sheet of newspaper as though you are going to read it. Starting at the bottom, roll up the sheet until it's 2 to 3 inches from the top edge. Place another newspaper over the top edge of the first sheet, being sure the two papers overlap. Continue rolling the paper, then add a third sheet of paper. Keep rolling and adding papers four more times. Roll the last piece of paper all the way up so that you have a long, skinny tube. Wrap a rubber band around

Storyteller TIPS

- For a neat treat, use chocolate candy coins wrapped in gold foil instead of paper coins!
- Younger kids especially will enjoy this lively Bible story. Invite your older class to share the story with younger children, then help them make the paper trees in Play It!

one end of the paper tube. Tape a piece of brown paper over one end of the tube near the rubber band. Then drop paper coins in the tube, making sure there's a coin for everyone in class and one for yourself. Use the picture of Daniel as Zacchaeus.

Set the scissors, picture of Zacchaeus, tape, and paper tube beside you, being careful not to reveal the hidden coins. Gather kids and ask them to tell about a time they were forgiven. Encourage children to tell what it felt like before and after they were forgiven. Then say: **Forgiveness is a very important part of loving Jesus. Today's Bible story is about a time Jesus forgave a short guy with an unusual name: Zacchaeus.** Hold up the picture of Zacchaeus. **You can help tell the story. Every time I say the word *Zacchaeus,* squat down low, then pop back up. And each time you hear the word *forgive, forgiven,* or *forgave,* jump up tall.**

Forgive and Forget

Now *Zacchaeus* wasn't just a short man; he was a grumpy, mean tax collector. He took people's money to pay taxes, but he always kept a bit for himself. The people never *forgave Zacchaeus* for stealing their money. They didn't like him and wouldn't *forgive* him. One day, Jesus was coming to town—everyone was excited. *Zacchaeus* had heard Jesus was able to *forgive* people. Could it be true? *Zacchaeus* wanted to see Jesus, but he was short and couldn't see over the crowd. How could he ever see Jesus?

Then *Zacchaeus* saw something that gave him an idea! What do you think *Zacchaeus* saw? Hold up the paper tube, being careful not to spill out the coins. Holding the tube carefully, make five 4-inch cuts into the end opposite the coins. Ask a volunteer to hold the bottom of the paper tube while you place your thumbs inside the tube and gradually pull the layers out. The tube will become taller and taller until it's about 6 feet tall! Then hold the paper tree up high and say: ***Zacchaeus* saw a tall tree, so he climbed up to peek at Jesus.** Tape Zacchaeus at the top of the tree. **Then *Zacchaeus* heard someone speak to him. "Zacchaeus! Zacchaeus!" said the voice. Who was talking to him? It was Jesus! Jesus wanted to go home with *Zacchaeus* to eat, so down the tree he scrambled.**

75

The people were amazed; some were even angry. "Why would Jesus want to eat with *Zacchaeus?*" they fussed. But as they ate, Jesus *forgave Zacchaeus* for the wrong things he'd done. *Zacchaeus* was so happy to be *forgiven* that he did an amazing thing! *Zacchaeus* opened his money bag (tear open the end of the paper tree and toss out the coins) and repaid the people all their money—and even more! Then the people *forgave Zacchaeus. Zacchaeus* was changed forever because Jesus had loved and *forgiven* him. Yeah, *Zacchaeus!*

Set aside the paper tree and have each child take a paper coin as a reminder of how Zacchaeus was forgiven and changed. Then ask:
- **How is Jesus' forgiveness a demonstration of his love?**
- **In what ways does Jesus' forgiveness change us?**
- **Why is it important for us to forgive others?**

Read aloud Matthew 6:14, 15. Say: **Loving others means we forgive them. It may not always be easy to forgive others, but Jesus wants us to be forgiving. Jesus says if we forgive others, God will forgive us! That's pretty great, isn't it? Let's make forgiveness bouquets to remind us of the importance of forgiveness.**

PLAY IT!

Have children form groups of three or four. Pair younger children with older kids for help in making the paper trees. Demonstrate how to make the tall paper trees (which are actually paper bouquets in this activity). When the fronds of the treetop are cut and the tree is pulled out to its full length, invite kids to make colorful construction-paper flowers to tape on the ends of the fronds. Suggest that children tear out green construction-paper leaves to tape to the tall stem of the pretend bouquet.

As kids work, encourage them to visit about times they found it difficult to forgive someone and how it felt to finally forgive that person. Have them discuss why it is important to ask for forgiveness and how that shows humility and willingness to change.

Finish the forgiveness bouquets by adding construction-paper cards that ask for forgiveness. Cards might read, "I was wrong. Can you forgive me?" or "Please forgive me. I want to change." Have younger children dictate their sentences to the older children to write. Challenge kids to think of someone they might give their bouquets to or encourage them to keep the bouquets to use when needed.

Say: **Zacchaeus discovered that an important part of being forgiven is not repeating the wrong behavior. When Jesus forgives us, we want to change. Changing isn't always easy, but it is important! Let's end with a prayer thanking Jesus for his forgiveness and asking for his help in changing.**

PRAY IT!

Have children remain in their small groups. Join hands and offer this prayer: **Dear Lord, we're so thankful for your loving forgiveness. We ask that you give us the courage to ask for forgiveness when we need it and the strength to change our ways when we're forgiven. Please help us be more forgiving to those around us. Just as you are forgiving, we want to be forgiving too. Amen.** Lead everyone in singing this song to the tune of "Jesus Loves Me."

Jesus loves me this I know.
He forgives me, it is so.
When I ask it from my heart,
His forgiveness always starts.
Yes, Jesus loves me.
Yes, Jesus loves me.
Yes, Jesus loves me—
And he forgives me too.

REPLAY IT!

Use this happy idea to reinforce and enrich the lesson!

● Celebrate Jesus' forgiveness with these lovely flower reminders. Tape golden chocolate coins to sturdy florist's wire, then add torn paper leaves to the wire stems. Use markers to decorate paper cups, then stuff modeling dough in the cups. Poke the stems of the forgiveness flowers in the dough, then add a decorated gift card with this poem:

Zacchaeus knew it;
We do too.
Forgiveness is golden
And meant for you!

Sow the Seeds!

Matthew 13:1-9; Psalm 119:16

What You'll Teach

We can learn God's Word.

What You'll Need

- For **Say It!** you'll need a Bible, permanent markers, a white plastic shower-curtain liner, scissors, an X-Acto knife, green ribbon, an envelope, construction paper, tape, and popped popcorn.
- For **Play It!** you'll need construction-paper flowers.
- For **Pray It!** you'll need markers, tape, and the construction-paper flowers used earlier.

Kid-Clue

You'll be using a decorated shower curtain to tell the parable of the sower and the seeds. Practice several times to be a super storyteller!

SAY IT!

Before the lesson, prepare the Bible-story mat as follows. Spread a white shower-curtain liner on the floor. (Shower curtain liners are very inexpensive and found in most discount stores.) Using the illustration on page 79 as a pattern, draw the rocks, the weeds, the path, and the garden rows on the shower curtain with permanent markers. Make the drawings large and very colorful. Ask an adult to cut a slit in the garden rows with an X-Acto knife, then turn the mat

Storyteller TIPS
Use Styrofoam packing peanuts or small paper wads instead of popped popcorn.

over. Tape an envelope under the slit with the open side facing the slit to make a secret pocket. Tape a paper flower to a 2-foot length of green ribbon, then tape the other end of the ribbon inside the pocket. Stuff the rest of the ribbon and the flower into the pocket, then turn the mat over. Pull the flower up through the slit as though it's growing, then replace the flower in its hiding place. Place popped popcorn in a bag and have it ready for the story.

Spread the mat on the floor and place the bag of popcorn beside you. Gather kids around the mat and ask everyone to name the most important thing anyone can learn. Some suggestions might include learning to talk, learning to walk, or learning to read. Then say: **Jesus told a story about the most important thing we can ever learn. His parable is about a farmer who planted some seeds. You can help sow popcorn seeds during the story.** Hand each person a small handful of popcorn, but tell them not to toss the seeds just yet. Then tell the following story.

Sow the Seeds!

The farmer went out to plant his field one day. He tossed the seeds in the air! Have children toss the popcorn above the mat. **The seeds scattered and fell. Where did they fall? Let's see!**

Lead everyone across the path on the mat as you say: **Some of the seeds fell on the hard path, and birds came and ate it up.** Have kids pick up the popcorn on or near the path. Then lead the kids to the rocks. **Some of the seeds fell among the rocky ground, where there wasn't much soil. The seeds grew quickly, but when the hot sun came up, the small plants withered and died.** Have kids pick up popcorn on or near the rocks, then lead the kids to the weeds. **Some of the seeds fell among the weeds and thorns. Ouch! Some of the seeds grew, but the weeds grew faster and choked the little plants out.** Pick up popcorn in and around the weeds. Lead the kids to the garden rows. **Finally, some of the seeds fell on good soil! These seeds grew to**

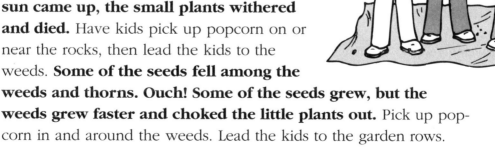

79

make many good plants—thirty times more than was planted! Reach in the secret pocket and pull up the long ribbon flower. **The harvest of the seeds on the good soil was huge!** Lead everyone in a lively round of applause.

Put the popcorn back in the bag, then ask:

● **Which seeds didn't grow well? Why?**

● **Which seeds grew best? Why?**

● **Which seeds in this story represent people who hear and learn God's Word? Explain.**

● **How can learning God's Word help us grow and produce good works?**

Say: **Jesus told this special story to teach about learning God's Word. In the story, the seeds represent God's Word, and we're the types of soil. Sometimes people hear God's Word, but they don't really listen and learn. This is what happens when the seeds dry up or blow away. Sometimes we hear God's Word and let others talk us out of our faith. This is what can happen to seeds that are choked among thorns. But when we hear, listen to, and learn from God's Word, we're like good soil that grows the fruit of God's love and wisdom!**

Read aloud Psalm 119:16. Then say: **The most important thing we can learn is God's Word and how to put God's Word to use in our lives. One way to do this is by reading the Bible and learning Scripture. Let's play a game that will help us learn a Scripture verse about God's Word.**

PLAY IT!

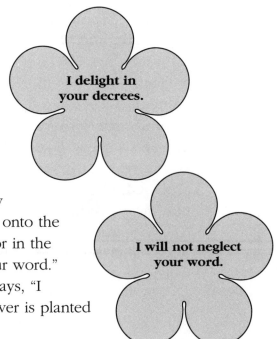

I delight in your decrees.

I will not neglect your word.

Hand everyone a paper flower. Explain that in this game, you'll work to learn Psalm 119:16, which says, "I delight in your decrees; I will not neglect your word."

Have children stand 2 feet away from the story mat, then invite four children to toss their flowers onto the mat. If a flower lands on the rocks, on the path, or in the weeds, the tosser must say, "I will not neglect your word." When a flower lands in the good soil, the tosser says, "I delight in your decrees." Play until everyone's flower is planted in the good soil.

Gather everyone and repeat Psalm 119:16 together. Then say: **If we neglect God's Word by not reading it, not thinking about it, or not obeying it, we can't grow good things in our lives, such as trust, faith, obedience, and wisdom. We want to learn God's Word because it's the most important thing we'll ever learn! Let's end with a prayer asking God to help us learn his Word.**

PRAY IT!

Hand each child a marker and a paper flower from *Play It!* Invite kids to draw smiley faces on the flowers, then write their names on the petals. As children work, remind them that learning God's Word takes commitment, time, patience, and practice—but that God's Word is worth it!

When the flowers are completed, hand each child a piece of tape. Then say: **After we pray, we'll tape our flowers to the good soil on the story mat to show how much we want to learn God's Word.** Pray: **Dear God, we thank you for your Word, which is the most important thing we can ever learn. Please help us have patience and perseverance as we read the Bible and learn your loving Word. In Jesus' name, amen.** As each child tapes her flower to the story mat, encourage her to repeat Psalm 119:16.

REPLAY IT!

To reinforce and enrich the lesson, try one of these great ideas!

● Plant unusual gardens for kids to take home and care for. For each garden, spread 1 inch of soil in a 9-by-11-inch aluminum cake pan. Use a pencil to write the word "Jesus" in the soil, then sprinkle radish seeds heavily in the furrows. Cover the soil and lightly sprinkle it with warm water. Caution children to keep the soil moist—not wet—and to place their gardens in sunny windows. The seeds will sprout within one week and soon spell out God's word for love!

● Form three groups and assign each one of the first three portions of Psalm 119 to read (vv. 1-8, 9-16, 17-24). Then have each group list the times God's Word and its importance is described. For example, verse 7 talks of learning God's laws, while verse 17 talks of obeying God's Word. Have groups share their discoveries with the whole group.

Build Your Faith!

Matthew 7:24-27; Psalm 62:1, 2, 5-8

What You'll Teach

The Lord is our foundation of faith.

What You'll Need

- For **Say It!** you'll need a Bible, construction paper, two large shoe boxes with lids, tape, markers, sandpaper, scissors, four large books or concrete blocks, and a large, heavy stone. Be sure the stone fits inside one of the boxes.
- For **Play It!** you'll need paper or newspaper, tape, and books.
- For **Pray It!** you'll need a Bible, markers, glue, felt, and large, flat stones.

Kid-Clue

You'll be using a trick box to tell the parable of the builders. Practice the story several times to be a super storyteller!

SAY IT!

Before the story, prepare the boxes to look like houses. Tape a red paper heart to the stone, then place it inside one of the boxes and make sure it stays over to one side. Tape sandpaper along the bottom edge of the other house so it appears to be built on sand. Place the boxes on top of the books or concrete blocks. If you're using books, they need to be the same size. Be sure the stone is resting on one of the books, but don't let kids see there's a stone inside!

Storyteller TIPS

During the story, be sure to pull away the correct book—the book that is not under the hidden stone in the house!

Gather children around the boxes and say: **When you build a house or other kind of building, it's important to plan where to build. In other words, you need to have a good strong foundation on which to build. Jesus told a parable about two builders—one who was foolish and one who was wise. When you hear me mention the *foolish builder,* make silent laughing motions. When you hear me mention the *wise builder,* point to your head and nod.**

Build Your Faith!

Once there were two men who wanted to build houses to live in. The *foolish builder* decided to build his house on the sand. Point to the house with the sand foundation. **But the *wise builder* chose to build his house on solid rock.** Point to the house with the hidden stone. **One day, a powerful storm blew in and with it, plenty of trouble! The rains fell, and the flood waters rose higher and higher. The wind blew and beat against the houses. Whose house do you think stood firm against all this trouble? Was it the *foolish builder's* house?** Point to the house with the sand foundation. **Or was it the *wise builder's* house?** Point to the house with the hidden stone. **Let's see!**

When the flood waters hit the *foolish builder's* house, the sand gave way and the house fell down! Crashhh! Pull one of the books from under the house with the sand foundation and let the house topple over. **But when the floods and wind struck the *wise builder's* house** (pull out the book that is not under the hidden stone—the house will not fall because the stone will keep it balanced on one book!) **the house stood firm—it didn't fall at all!** Kids will be amazed that the house stands firm, but don't give away the secret just yet. Say: **The *wise builder's* house withstood all the trouble because he had built his house on solid rock!**

Gently hold the house with the hidden stone and say: **What a great Bible story and such a good lesson! Jesus wanted us to** understand that faith in him is the firm foundation we need to build our lives on. In other words, when we have love for Jesus inside our hearts (open the box and remove the stone with the red paper heart), then our faith will see us through trouble. If we choose to build our faith on money, sports heroes, or anything other than Jesus, we'll be sure to fall down flat—like the foolish builder's house!

Then ask children to answer the following question:
● **How can we build stronger faith in Jesus?**
Read aloud Psalm 62:1, 2, 5-8, then say: **Let's see what kind of strong foundations we can build in a fun game.**

PLAY IT!

Have children form pairs. Hand each pair a couple of sheets of paper or newspaper and tape. Challenge them to invent paper supports that they believe will hold the weight of one or two books. Tell them to use tape and either fold, roll, or twist their papers to make cylinders, triangles, or squares that will support weight. Have them choose to make two supports or use both papers to make one support.

After the book supports are finished, use one or two books to test them. Each time a paper holds a book, have everyone clap and say, "Firm foundations are best!"

When all the supports have been tested, discuss what may happen if we choose to build our lives on someone or something other than Jesus. Then name ways that a strong foundation of faith can help us through troubles. Say: **When we rely on Jesus and have strong faith, we won't crumble apart when troubles come along. We'll stand firm. Did you know that the Bible often refers to the Lord as "our rock"? What do you think that means?** Allow children to tell their ideas, then say: **Let's end with a prayer thanking God for being our strong foundation and our rock and asking God's help in making our foundation of faith even stronger.**

PRAY IT!

Have everyone find a quiet place to sit. Read aloud Psalm 62:1, 2, 5-8. Then quietly pray: **Dear Lord, there is no one stronger or mightier than you. You are our rock and our salvation. You alone are our firm foundation. Please help us build our lives and our faith on you alone so we can stand firm when troubles come along. Thank you for your love, Lord. In Jesus' name, amen.**

Have each child choose a large flat stone. Help kids use markers to write "You're my rock and foundation" on the sides of the stones. Decorate the stones with heart shapes, crosses, or other shapes and designs. Finally, have kids glue several small pieces of felt to the bottoms of the stones to prevent them from scratching tables or shelves. Tell kids to take the stones home as reminders that the only foundation we want to build our lives on is the rock-solid love of Jesus Christ.

End by singing the following song to the tune of "This Is the Day That the Lord Has Made," echoing the words in italics. Sing in a lively but worshipful manner and encourage kids to think about the words they're singing.

You are my rock *(You are my rock)*
And my salvation. *(and my salvation.)*
And you alone *(And you alone)*
Are my foundation. *(are my foundation.)*
God is my fortress and my rock.
My faith in him will never stop, oh
You are my rock *(You are my rock)*
And my salvation.

REPLAY IT!

For lesson reinforcement and enrichment, try one of these fun ideas!

● Make delicious pretend rocks to nibble. Let children dip large marshmallows in milk, then roll the marshmallows in toasted shredded coconut. Mmm good!

● Children love building, so turn them loose with scraps or wood, craft sticks, foil, paper, old springs, wire, and wood glue. Encourage kids to work in pairs and to help each other glue their creations. Provide large stones or bricks for children to set their creative efforts on, then invite another class in for a tour of your buildings. Have your class remind the other class that we want to build our faith on the rock-solid love of Jesus!

The Good Samaritan

Luke 10:30-37; Ephesians 4:32

What You'll Teach

We can help others.

What You'll Need

- For **Say It!** you'll need tape, scissors, construction paper, and a 3-by-24-inch length of white ribbon. You'll also need a photocopy of the men and donkey silhouettes from page 112.
- For **Play It!** you'll need scissors, tape, 3-inch-wide white ribbon, construction paper, and photocopies of the man and donkey silhouettes from page 112. You'll need one photocopy for each child.
- For **Pray It!** you'll need no extra supplies.

Kid-Clue

You'll be using a story ribbon to tell the parable of the Good Samaritan. Practice several times to be a super storyteller!

SAY IT!

Before story time, make a photocopy of the silhouette patterns of the donkey and the men. You'll need four men and one donkey. Cut out the silhouettes. On one of the men, glue a red construction-paper belt. (This is the priest). On another, glue a yellow hat. (This will be the Levite.) And on another man, glue a blue stripe along the hem of his robe. (This is the Samaritan.)

Storyteller TIPS

Tape the bottom of your story ribbon to the wall so it will hang straight as you tell the Bible story.

Tape or pin the ribbon to a wall or bulletin board. Place the figures and the tape beside you. Have kids form five groups and sit near the white ribbon. Ask them to tell about times they've helped someone. Encourage children to tell how it felt being a special helper. Then say: **Jesus wants us to help others. In fact, Jesus taught us about helping in a special story called the parable of the Good Samaritan. You can help tell the story.** Point to a group. **This group can play the part of the hurt man. Whenever you hear about the hurt man, quickly lie down and make soft groaning noises.** Point to another group. **This group can be the priests. When I mention the priest, walk slowly with heads bowed and say, "Not me."** Point to another group. **This group will be the Levites. Whenever I mention the Levite, walk slowly with heads bowed and say, "Not me."** Point to another group. **This group will be the donkey. Whenever I mention the donkey, trot and say, "Hee-haw!"** Point to another group. **And this group will be the Good Samaritans. When I mention the Good Samaritan, jump up and say, "I'll help!" Ready? Let's hear the story!**

The Good Samaritan

Once long ago, there was a man walking on the road. Hold the man without decorations toward the top of the ribbon. **Robbers came and beat him and left the *hurt man* in the road.** Tape the hurt man in a prone position at the top of the ribbon. **Soon, a *priest* came walking along the road.** Tape the priest with the red belt below the hurt man on the ribbon. **Would the *priest* stop and help the *hurt man?* Nope, the *priest* just walked by! Then a *Levite* came walking along the road.** Tape the Levite with the yellow hat below the priest. **Would the *Levite* stop and help the *hurt man?* Nope, the *Levite* walked by!**

The *hurt man* didn't think anyone would help him! But then a *donkey* came trotting along. Tape the donkey below the Levite. **Riding the *donkey* was a man from Samaria—also known as a *Samaritan*.** Hold the Samaritan beside the hurt man. ***Samaritans*** **weren't supposed to talk with Israelites, and the *hurt man* was from**

87

Jerusalem. He was an Israelite! Do you think the *Samaritan* stopped to help the *hurt man?* **Yes!** Tape the Samaritan beside the hurt man.

The *Good Samaritan* cleaned the *hurt man's* wounds and carried him to town on his *donkey.* Then the *Good Samaritan* even paid for the *hurt man* to stay at the inn! The *priest* and the *Levite* didn't help the *hurt man,* but the *Good Samaritan* did! Hooray for the *Good Samaritan* and his help!

Thank the children for their help telling the story, then ask:
- **Why do you think the Samaritan stopped to help the man?**
- **In what way did the Samaritan show his love?**
- **What can we learn from Jesus' parable?**

Say: **The Good Samaritan was the least likely one to help the man, yet he was the only one who helped! Jesus wants us to know we can help others no matter what. When we help, we demonstrate our caring and our love—not just for others, but for Jesus too. Let's help each other make story ribbons so we can remember the goodness of the Good Samaritan.**

PLAY IT!

Be sure you have a 2-foot length of ribbon for each child. Hand each child one photocopy of the silhouette patterns. Direct kids to cut out the silhouettes. Explain that they'll need four men and one donkey. Have children add construction paper belts, hats, and stripes to the silhouette figures, then tape them to their ribbons so they can retell the Bible story. Use the story ribbon from *Say It!* as a pattern, and encourage children to help each other with their projects.

As children work, read aloud Ephesians 4:32. Then visit about times they may have shown kindness by helping someone in need. Ask questions such as "How does Jesus help us every day?" "How can we help others who may need us?" and "Why do you think Jesus wants us to be helpful and kind?"

If there's time, have children form pairs and use their story ribbons to retell the Bible story. Then say: **Let's use our story ribbons to offer a prayer asking God to show us ways to help and be kind to others.**

PRAY IT!

Have children sit in a circle holding their story ribbons. Before you pray, have them point to each human silhouette and think of one person they could pledge to help in the upcoming week. Suggest family members, friends, neighbors, and people at school or church. Ask children to name ways we can help others, then say: **There are many ways to help others. We may help by giving time, money, talents, or even through prayer. It's not important how we help, but it is important *that* we help! See if you can help each of the people you thought of during the coming week. Now let's ask God's help in showing us ways to be kind and thoughtful.**

Pray: **Dear God, thank you for all the help you give us every day and in every way. Please show us ways we can help those around us. Let us be on the lookout for times someone needs us as friends or as encouragers. And help us remember to pray for others and to offer them help through talking to you. Amen.**

Encourage kids to hang their story ribbons in their rooms to remind them of their pledges to help others this week.

REPLAY IT!

Use one of these ideas to reinforce and enrich today's lesson!

● Offer to help a needy child with school supplies even if it's the middle of the school year! Encourage children to bring in things they think a child in school would need, such as new pencils, scissors, crayons, or a paperback dictionary. Place the donations in a new notebook and present the gift to a local school to give a needy child.

● Show children that help can travel around the world through their prayers. If your church sponsors a missionary, begin a Prayer-Care week and challenge children to pray for that missionary and his people for the next week. Remind children that the Samaritan didn't come from the hurt man's country but helped the man anyway. Take time for the class to write the missionary and his family, thanking them for traveling around the world to help others in God's name.

Take Time for God

Luke 10:38-42; Matthew 6:33

What You'll Teach

We can take time for God.

What You'll Need

- For **Say It!** you'll need a Bible and two large scarves or towels.
- For **Play It!** you'll need pencils with erasers, a penny for each child in class, and photocopies of Matthew 6:33.
- For **Pray It!** you'll need no extra supplies.

Kid-Clue

You'll be using actions and rhyme to tell the story of Mary and Martha. Practice the story with a friend to be a super storyteller!

SAY IT!

If you have two storytellers for this Bible story, decide who will read the part of Martha and who will read the part of Mary. Have Martha place the scarf around her waist as an apron and Mary drape the scarf over her head as a headdress.

Gather children in two groups, one to follow Martha's actions and one to follow Mary's. Have the groups sit on opposite sides of the rooms. Ask kids to tell about things they do during the day or on the weekends that keep them busy. Then say: **There are always so many things that**

Storyteller TIPS

This story works well with two children playing the parts of Martha and Mary. Simply read the poem in parts as you lead the class in the accompanying actions.

keep us busy! School, music lessons, homework, household chores, and playing with friends take up a lot of time. But what things are really important to make time for? Two of Jesus' friends learned what was important for them to do. Follow along with our actions as we tell the story of Mary and Martha. Then see if you can figure out the important thing we should make time for.

Take Time for God

MARTHA:

The floor needs sweeping; *(Make sweeping motions.)*
Oh, let's scrub the pans! *(Make scrubbing motions.)*
Then we'll shake out the rugs as fast as we can! *(Shake out rugs.)*
I'll make the beds, *(Plump up pillows.)*
And you clean the rest. *(Pretend to dust.)*
Jesus is here and we want it the best! *(Put arms in the air.)*
Come on now, Mary, it's really your turn . . . *(Point to Mary.)*

MARY:

But I want to stay here to listen and learn. *(Sit and nod.)*
I want to hear Jesus and not hesitate—*(Look upward.)*
The floors and the pans, Martha, really can wait! *(Nod head slowly.)*

MARTHA:

But Mary, the house is truly a wreck—*(Shake head "No!")*
Let's dust the shelves 'til there's no little speck! *(Make dusting motions.)*
Let's clean and let's scrub as quick as we can *(Make scrubbing motions.)*
'Til the house is shiny and all spick-n-span! *(Put arms in the air.)*

MARY:

Dear Martha, please sit down here with us. *(Sit peacefully.)*
The house is just fine—there's no need to fuss. *(Shake your head "No.")*

91

Nothing's as dear as this moment in time;
To listen to Jesus is perfect and fine. *(Look upward.)*
Listen Martha! Jesus is speaking to you. *(Cup hands behind ears.)*
He's saying that this is the place now for you. *(Point beside you.)*
So leave all the housework—just give it a nod. *(Nod your head.)*
Come here to listen and take time for God! *(Smile and point upward.)*

Have children sit together, then ask:

● **Who do you think was spending her time wisely? Explain.**

● **Why is it important to take time for God?**

● **How can we spend time with God?**

Read aloud Matthew 6:33. Then say: **There's nothing more important to do with our time than spend it with God! Too many times we think we're too busy to pray or read the Bible or go to church, but taking time out with God is the best spent time we can have. Let's play a lively game to remind us how important every minute with God is.**

PLAY IT!

Before game time, make one photocopy of this verse for each child: "But seek first his kingdom" (Matthew 6:33).

Form two groups, but don't let either group know what the other will be doing. Hand one group the papers with Matthew 6:33 on them. (Save the rest of the verses for *Pray It!*) Instruct this group to try to memorize the verse and reference in the allotted time. Then hand the other group pencils with erasers and enough pennies so each person in class can have one. Tell this group to shine all the pennies by rubbing them with the erasers. Let the groups work for about 3 minutes, then call time.

Ask each group to tell what they have been doing for the last several minutes. Have the group with the money display the shiny pennies and the Scripture group repeat the verse. Then ask:

● **Which group spent their time more wisely? Why?**

● **Why is it wise to choose time to learn about God?**

Say: **Time spent with God or learning about God and his Word is time invested in eternity. Shiny pennies may be pretty, but they'll soon tarnish, and the time spent cleaning them will have been for nothing. But what we gain from learning God's Word or praying or reading the Bible will last forever. Yes!** Have kids give each other high fives. Then say: **The time we spend with God is the most valuable time of all. So let's spend time with God right now in prayer.**

PRAY IT!

Give each child a penny and a Scripture paper. Invite children to find quiet places to sit. Say: **You are holding pennies that represent time we spend away from God. You're also holding Scripture verses that represent the time we choose to spend with God. Take a few moments with God right now to think of all the ways you can choose to spend your time this week. Then talk to God and ask him to show you ways to spend more time with him each day—even if it's only 10 minutes. There is a lot we do to waste time, but even one minute with God is never a waste!**

Allow several minutes of silent time, then say: **See if you can spend time today learning the verse on your paper. Keep the penny as a reminder of how golden time is with God!**

REPLAY IT!

To reinforce and enrich today's lesson, try this great idea!

● Make Scripture sundials to remind kids to spend time with God. For each sundial, wrap two craft sticks in a crisscross pattern with colorful yarn. Decorate a plastic plate with permanent markers or paint pens. Then write a Scripture verse such as Matthew 6:33 or Psalm 119:16 around the edge of the plate. Place a walnut-sized piece of florist's clay in the center of the plastic plate. Poke the craft stick cross in the center of the clay. Place the Scripture sundial in a sunny place indoors or out. Each time children look at the dial, see if they can repeat the verse around the edges. In no time at all, they'll have the verse memorized!

True Talents

Matthew 25:29; Galatians 5:13

What You'll Teach

We can use our talents to serve others.

What You'll Need

- For **Say It!** you'll need a Bible, a dish tub, newspapers, sand, and a plastic coin for each child in class.
- For **Play It!** you'll need small sandwich bags, a variety of dried beans, baby food jars with lids, Tacky craft glue, ribbon, index cards, tape, and markers. You'll also need photocopies of the bean soup recipe on page 96.
- For **Pray It!** you'll need no extra supplies.

Kid-Clue

You'll be using a pan full of sand and prizes to tell the parable of the talents. Practice the story several times to be a super storyteller!

SAY IT!

Before class, fill a dish tub with sand and bury all but one plastic coin. Set the tub on newspapers on the floor in the storytelling area.

Gather kids around the tub and ask them to tell about special talents they may have and how they use those talents. Some talents might include singing, being extra good in math class, being able to blow big bubbles, or excelling in some sport. Then say: **God gives each of us special talents to**

Storyteller TIPS

If you can't find plastic coins, use shiny pennies or gold foil-wrapped chocolate coins instead.

use, and it's up to us how we're going to use them. **Today's Bible story is a story Jesus told about using what God gives us. In this story, talents are coins.** Hold up a plastic coin, then tell the following story.

True Talents

One day, a master called his three servants to him. The master gave one servant five talents. He gave another servant two talents. And he gave the third servant one talent. Then the master left on a journey. What would you do with the money? Allow children to tell their ideas, then continue.

The first servant invested his five talents and received five more. The servant with two talents gained two more. But the servant with one talent went and buried his coin. Bury the plastic coin in the sand. **What do you think happened when the master returned? The first servant said, "Master, I took the five talents you gave me and gained five more!" "Well done, good and faithful servant," said the master. Then the second servant said, "Master, I took the two talents you gave me and earned two more!" "Well done, good and faithful servant," said the master. Then the servant who buried his coin dug it up and gave it to his master.**

Dig out a plastic coin and hold it up. **This servant said, "I buried this coin to keep it safe, since I know you are a hard man." But the master said, "You lazy servant! I trusted you with a coin and you did nothing to use it, nothing to make it gain more! Give that coin to the servant with ten, for whoever has will be given more!" And the servant with one talent now had none.**

What does this story mean? It means that when God gives something to us, we're to put what he gives us to use for him. When we serve others with the talents God gives us, we're really serving God! God trusts us with special talents, and we

shouldn't bury them like the servant in the story. We want to use them to serve God. Now, let's each dig up a coin to remind us not to hide our talents!

Invite children to dig in the sand for the coins. When each child has a coin, ask:
● **How is serving others a way to serve God?**
● **How can we use our time, talents, gifts, and money to help others?**
Set aside the coins. Read aloud Galatians 5:13, then say: **When we serve and give to others, we're using the gifts God has given us. Let's see what happens when we give to others.**

PLAY IT!

Hand each child a sandwich bag containing a variety of dried beans. Explain that the beans are pretend coins and that the object of this game is to give away all your coins before time is called. Point out that any time you receive a coin from someone, you must give that person two more coins in return.

Play for 3 minutes, then call time and ask what happened when the coins were given away. Then say: **This game is like using the blessings God gives us. When we share those blessings and use them for God's service, God multiplies our blessings and gives us more! So let's use these pretty beans to serve God right now. We'll make miniature soup starters to feed hungry people.**

Have children form pairs and hand each pair a baby food jar and lid. Set out ribbon, Tacky craft glue, index cards, tape, and markers. Instruct partners to combine their beans and pour them into the jars. Add more beans as needed. Replace the lids and glue ribbon around them. Photocopy the following directions and glue them on the index cards. Tape the cards to the bottoms of the jars.

 # Bean Soup Starter

Rinse the beans, then boil them in 3 cups of salted water until tender. Add 1 cup of rice and 1 cup of chopped ham, cooked hamburger, or cubed chicken. Add salt and pepper to taste. Simmer the soup for at least 30 minutes.

96

When the soup-starter jars are done, say: **Let's see what the Bible says about what happens when we use what God gives us to serve him.** Read aloud Matthew 25:29. Then say: **God promises to entrust us with even more when we use what he gives us. That's pretty awesome, isn't it? Let's end with a prayer thanking God for his gifts to us and asking for God's help in using what he has given us to serve him and others.** Donate the soup-starter jars to a local food pantry or other service organization.

PRAY IT!

Quickly bury the plastic coins in the sand once more. Gather children near the sand tub, then say: **Let's join hands and pray. Then we'll each dig up a coin and name one talent we have that we can use this week to serve God.** Pray: **Dear God, thank you for the talents and gifts you lovingly give to us. We know how precious your gifts are, and we don't want to waste them or hide them away. Please help us continually find new ways of using our talents to serve you and others. In Jesus' name we pray, amen.**

Take turns digging up plastic coins and telling talents that could be used during the coming week to serve God and others. Challenge kids to also tell how their talents will be used. Then end by reminding children to take home their coins and to leave them in the open for everyone to see and be encouraged about using their God-given gifts!

REPLAY IT!

Try this fun idea for lesson reinforcement and enrichment!

● Have children form pairs or trios. Hand each group a large sheet of paper and colored markers. Have children write the word "serve" down the left-hand side of the papers. Challenge groups to list ways of serving God and others that begin with each letter in the word serve. For example, one way to serve might be "singing" in the choir at church. Another way might be "encouraging" someone who feels sad or lonely. When all the groups are done, let them read their lists to the entire class. Display the papers in a hallway where everyone can be reminded of all the different ways we can put God's gifts to work.

Jesus Is Alive!

Matthew 28:7, 8; Mark 16:6

What You'll Teach

Jesus is alive.

What You'll Need

- For **Say It!** you'll need a paper plate, a sheet of paper, and scissors.
- For **Play It!** you'll need plastic pull-apart Easter eggs.
- For **Pray It!** you'll need permanent markers, pencils, slips of paper, and a basket.

Kid-Clue

You and a friend will use scissors and paper to tell the Easter story. Practice the story several times to be super storytellers!

SAY IT!

Storyteller TIPS

Before class, practice folding and snipping the paper several times as you tell the different parts of the story.

You'll need two storytellers for this Bible presentation. Decide who will tell the first part of the story and who will tell the second part. You and your friend will want to practice cutting out the story shapes, so plan a bit of practice time! The person telling the first part of the story will be cutting a half sheet of paper into shapes to tell about the Last Supper and Jesus' death on the cross. The other person will cut a paper plate to tell the story of the first Easter morning. Read the story to know what to say and follow the illustrations and directions to know how to fold and cut the story shapes.

Gather children and say: **The saddest story ever told and the happiest story ever told are both found in the Bible. In fact, they're found right next to each**

other in all four Gospels! Let's hear the saddest and the happiest stories ever told as we cut our way back through time to Jesus' last days on earth.

Jesus Is Alive!

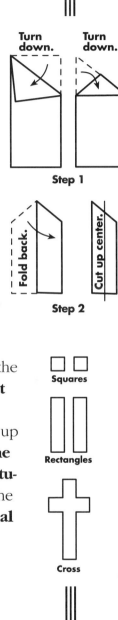

Step 1

Turn down. Turn down.

Fold back. Cut up center.

Step 2

☐ ☐
Squares

||
Rectangles

✝
Cross

Part 1: The Saddest Story Ever Told

As you tell the story, fold the half sheet of paper according to the illustration. Form the house shape (step 1), then say: **Jesus and his disciples were in Jerusalem. It was time for the Passover Feast, and they were all gathered in the upper room of a house.** Hold up the house shape, then fold it backward lengthwise and cut up the center (step 2). **The disciples didn't know it would be their last supper together, but Jesus knew that he would soon die to forgive the sins of the world. Jesus picked up the bread** (hold up one of the little squares), **blessed and broke it, and said "Take and eat. This is my body."** Tear the square in half. **Then Jesus took the cup** (hold up the other little square), **gave thanks, and said, "Drink, for this is my blood poured out for you."** Tip the square, then set it down. **Then Jesus wrapped a towel around his waist** (hold up one of the rectangle shapes) **and washed his disciples' feet, explaining that we are all to serve one another. After this last supper, Jesus went to the Garden of Gethsemane to pray under a tree.** Hold up the other rectangle shape. **But during Jesus' prayer, soldiers came to arrest him. They took him to town for trial, and Jesus eventually died on the cross to pay for our sins.** Unfold and hold up the cross shape. **Jesus died so we could be forgiven and have eternal life with him. It was the saddest day Jesus' friends ever knew. But did the sadness end there? Oh, no!**

Part 2: The Happiest Story Ever Told

Fold the paper plate in half as you say: **Jesus' body was laid in a cave-like tomb and sealed shut with a large stone. Jesus' disciples and friends were so sad. They stayed together, praying and crying. Then on the morning of the third day, Jesus'**

99

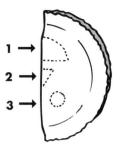

mother, Mary, and his friend Mary went to the tomb.
What do you suppose they saw? Cut the stone from the
paper plate (step 1). **The huge stone had been rolled away
from the tomb!** Unfold and hold up the cut piece (the paper
stone), then cut out and hold up the angel shape (step 2).
**Then they saw a bright white angel! The angel said,
"Jesus is not here. He is risen!" Mary poked her head into
the tomb for a peek.** Carefully poke your scissors through
the paper plate and cut out a circle (step 3). Hold up the two
circles and say: **Mary couldn't believe her eyes! The tomb
really was empty! Jesus is alive! Both Marys were so
happy!** Open the paper plate to reveal a happy face, then say:
**They were so happy, they ran to tell the rest of Jesus' disci-
ples that Jesus is alive!**

Set aside the scissors and cutouts, then ask:

● **Why was this the saddest story ever told? Why is it the happiest?**

● **In what ways was Jesus' death the greatest demonstration of love the
world has ever known?**

● **How can we receive Jesus' forgiveness and eternal life?**

Say: **Jesus died to forgive our sins. And we can be forgiven if we ask for
Jesus' forgiveness, then love, follow, and obey him. Easter is a time of celebra-
tion because we know that Jesus is alive. Let's play a game to remind us of the
joy both Marys felt when they saw the stone rolled away and knew that Jesus
had conquered death!**

PLAY IT!

Hand each child a plastic pull-apart egg. Then have children form two teams and
line up facing each other. Explain that in this relay-style game, the first person will roll
an egg on the floor to the child opposite her. When she reaches the other line, she
must shout "Jesus is alive" to share the good news with that person. Then that player
is to roll his egg across to the next person and shout the news.

Start one child from opposite ends of both lines. Continue zigging and zagging and
telling the good news until everyone has rolled his egg. Then play again, but this time
toss the eggs instead of rolling them. For even more fun, invite children to invent their

own ways of relaying eggs and the good news to each other.

Gather kids and read aloud Mark 16:6 and Matthew 28:7, 8. Then discuss why it's important to tell others that Jesus is alive and wants to forgive them. Ask children why they think telling others about Jesus is called the "good news." Then say: **Let's end with a prayer thanking God for Jesus' love and for dying on the cross for our sins.**

PRAY IT!

Invite children to use permanent markers to decorate their plastic eggs. Then hand out slips of paper and pencils and ask children to write reasons they're happy that Jesus is alive. Reasons might include because Jesus loves us, can forgive us, or helps us. Place the slips of paper inside the eggs, then place the eggs in a basket.

Gather children around the basket. Say: **It's especially important at this time of year to thank God for sending us his Son and offering us a chance to be forgiven. Let's say a prayer, then share some of the reasons we know, love, and follow Jesus.** Pray: **Dear Lord, there aren't enough words to thank you for the loving gift of Jesus. He died on the cross so we might live; he suffered so we could be happy. We're so glad Jesus rose to new life and is alive today! Thank you for Jesus, and thank you for his wonderful love. Amen.** Take turns opening the plastic eggs and reading the slips of paper. Replace the papers in the eggs, then let children take their eggs home as reminders of Jesus' love and their love for Jesus.

REPLAY IT!

Use this Easter idea to reinforce and enrich the lesson!

● Show children how to fold and cut the paper plate to tell the story of Jesus' resurrection and the joy of the first Easter morning. Let children cut their own plates, then decorate the smiling paper faces with fabric, yarn, glitter glue, markers, crayons, and other crafty tidbits. Help children write "He has risen" (Matthew 28:7) on the backs of the plates. Encourage children to present this fold-n-snip devotion at home and for their friends as they remind everyone that Jesus is alive!

Homeward to Heaven

Luke 24:33-53; Mark 16:15

What You'll Teach

We can tell others about Jesus.

What You'll Need

- For **Say It!** you'll need scissors, fishing line, pushpins or thumb tacks, a bulletin board, construction paper, markers, fiberfill, tape, and an old Bible-story coloring book.
- For **Play It!** you'll need paper, markers, and rubber bands.
- For **Pray It!** you'll need no extra supplies.

Kid-Clue

You'll be using an action bulletin board to tell the story of Jesus' ascension. Practice telling the story to be a super storyteller!

SAY IT!

Storyteller TIPS

If you don't have a bulletin board, use a piece of foam board or an acoustic ceiling panel.

Before the lesson, prepare the bulletin board as follows. Cover the board with blue paper (or cloud-patterned wrapping paper). Place fringed green construction paper along the bottom of the display and add a few green hills and a brown mountain. Add a twisted crepe-paper border if you desire. Be sure you have pushpins or thumb tacks instead of straight pins. Pushpins have large heads on them, which will help your characters stay in place. Color and cut out pictures of Jesus and of several of his disciples from a Bible-story coloring book.

Position a pushpin at the top right corner of the bulletin board. Put another push-pin at the center top of the bulletin board. (See illustration.) Cut a 5-foot piece of fishing line and tape a pushpin to one end. Tape the figure of Jesus on the other end. Run the fishing line up and over both pushpins so the figure of Jesus hangs down in the center of the bulletin board. Pin the figure of Jesus in place, then poke the pushpin on the end of the fishing line in place. When you unpin the figure of Jesus and gently pull on the pin attached to the fishing line, Jesus will rise upward. Neat, isn't it?

Place the fiberfill, figures, and pushpins beside you. Gather kids in front of the bulletin board and ask them to tell about important messages they may have told. Then say: **Today's Bible story is about a very important message that Jesus told us to tell others. Jesus was leaving and wanted to be sure we got the message. So listen to the story, and when you know what that message is, give a clap. When you know where Jesus is going, give two claps.**

Homeward to Heaven

Point to the figure of Jesus and say: **After Jesus rose from the tomb, he talked with his disciples.** Slowly pin the pictures of the disciples to the bulletin board. **Jesus told his disciples to meet him by a mountain outside Jerusalem. So the disciples were gathered by the mountain, and they waited for Jesus. It was a beautiful day with lots of clouds in the sky, and as the disciples waited, they wondered what Jesus would tell them.** Loosely pin fiberfill at the top of the display, below the center pushpin. Be sure to leave a gap for the figure of Jesus to rise through.

When the disciples saw Jesus, they worshiped him. Unpin the figure of Jesus. **Then Jesus gave them a very important command. Jesus told his disciples to go into all the world and to tell everyone the good news about forgiveness and eternal life. Jesus wanted them to teach other people the truth and how to obey God. Jesus told them to baptize**

others in the name of the Father and Son and Holy Spirit. Then something amazing happened! Carefully unpin the pushpin on the end of the fishing line. Gently pull the line downward to make the Jesus figure go upward into the clouds. **Jesus was lifted to heaven through the clouds! Jesus had gone to heaven to sit at the right hand of God!** When the Jesus figure is in the clouds, stop pulling and pin the pushpin in place. **And what did the disciples do? They obeyed Jesus! They went to tell everyone the good news about Jesus—and we can too!**

Then ask children the following questions:
- **Why do you think Jesus wants us to tell others about him?**
- **How can we spread the good news about Jesus?**
- **Who are people we can tell about Jesus' love and forgiveness?**
- **In what ways is telling others about Jesus like spreading love?**

Say: **Jesus wants us to tell others about him. Jesus wants us to tell others that they can be forgiven and live in heaven with him forever. The disciples obeyed Jesus, but they found out that it's not always easy to get the word through! Let's play a game about getting the message about Jesus through to others.**

PLAY IT!

Before game time, write the following on a piece of paper: "Go into all the world and preach the good news to all creation" (Mark 16:15). Make three photocopies of the paper, then roll them like scrolls and fasten them with rubber bands.

Choose three children to be messengers and hand each a scroll. Choose one child to be a receiver. Have the rest of the children form a circle with the receiver standing in the center. Position the messengers outside the circle. Explain that in this game, the messengers must try to get their scrolls through to the receiver by passing, tossing, or scooting them. The players in the circle are to try to block the scrolls from getting through. Play continues for 3 minutes or until all the scrolls get through. Play several times, choosing new receivers and messengers each time.

When the game is finished, have children give each other high fives for trying so hard. Then invite children to sit in a circle. Ask a volunteer to read aloud one of the scrolls, then discuss what obstacles might keep us from getting the good news about Jesus to others.

Say: **It may not always be easy to tell others about Jesus, but we want to keep trying. The good news is worth it! And Jesus wants us to spread the news. Let's end with a prayer asking Jesus to help us spread the joyous news about his love and forgiveness to others.**

PRAY IT!

Have children spread out around the room. Challenge them to take a moment to think of something about Jesus they could tell someone, such as Jesus loves you, Jesus wants to forgive you, and you can have a fresh new life with Jesus. Then say: **Let's take turns telling each other something about Jesus. When you've told someone, link arms with that person, then go tell someone else. We'll continue until everyone is joined.**

When everyone is joined, pray: **Dear Lord, there is no greater news than the good news about your love and forgiveness. We want the whole world to know, love, and follow you. Please help us spread the good news to others. In Jesus' name we pray, amen.**

Challenge children to tell one person about Jesus this week. Have each child whisper that person's name to the child beside her.

REPLAY IT!

Try this fun idea for lesson reinforcement and enrichment!

● Hand each child a pen, three index cards, and three stamps. (Buy postcard stamps.) Encourage children to write one or two sentences about Jesus on each card, then address the cards to friends and family members, and add stamps. Have a phone book handy for research! Decorate the cards if you wish, then take a walk to a nearby mailbox or to the mail drop in the church office to mail your cards. Remind kids that it only takes a few minutes to let others know how wonderful and life-saving knowing Jesus can be!

A Heavenly Hope

Revelation 21:1–22:5; John 14:2, 3

What You'll Teach

Jesus is preparing a place for us in heaven.

What You'll Need

- For **Play It!** you'll need permanent markers, colored electrical tape, scissors, fiberfill, staplers, and 8- or 10-inch squares of white craft felt. You'll need two squares for each child.
- For **Say It!** you'll need a blank overhead transparency, water, food coloring, cotton swabs, and paper towels. You'll also need an overhead projector.
- For **Pray It!** you'll need a blank overhead transparency, a marker, and an overhead projector.

Kid-Clue

You'll be using the overhead projector to tell what heaven will be like. Practice the story several times to be a super storyteller!

PLAY IT!

For this lesson, you'll present the craft activity before the Bible story. The heavenly headrest pillows you make will be used when you listen to the Bible story later.

Hand each child two squares of white craft felt. Provide scissors, colored electrical tape, permanent markers, fiberfill, and staplers. Explain that you'll be making heavenly pillows on which kids can rest their heads during the Bible story later. Then show kids how to put one felt square on top of the other and then staple around three sides and a portion of the fourth. Stuff the pillows with several handfuls of fiberfill, then finish stapling the fourth side. Stick a tape border around the pillow edges to cover the staples. Encourage children to use permanent markers or colored tape to decorate their heavenly pillows with peaceful designs such as clouds, stars, hearts, or flowers.

As kids work, ask them to imagine what heaven will be like. Mention that today's Bible story is about heaven and what the Bible tells us about what heaven will be like.

When the pillows are finished, have children hold them up so others can see their handiwork. Then say: **Jesus went to live in heaven, and he has promised to prepare places for us too. But what will heaven be like? Will it be pretty and peaceful? Will there be flowers and streams? Let's rest our heads and find out what the Bible says about the new heaven we can share with Jesus!**

SAY IT!

Before the story, set up the overhead projector and aim it so it will shine images on the ceiling. Place a blank transparency on the overhead and set cotton swabs, paper towels, the food coloring drop-bottles, and a small bowl of water next to the overhead. (Use a small table or chair to hold your special storytelling items.) Keep the overhead off until it's time for the story.

Invite children to find places to lie on the floor with their heads on their pillows. Say: **The Bible gives us clues as to what the new heaven and earth will be like. Let's take a make-believe trip to see what the Bible says the new heaven will be like.** Turn on the overhead projector. Follow the directions and the illustration to know when to add food coloring and when to smear or paint the colors with cotton swabs.

A Heavenly Hope

Dribble blue and red drops at the top of the transparency, then mix them with a cotton swab to make swirly purple clouds while you say: **The holy city will come down out of heaven from God. It will be shining and bright like the most beautiful of jewels!** Drizzle small drops of yellow under the clouds and around the edges of the transparency to make walls as you say: **The city** will be surrounded by high walls with twelve gates. There will be three gates on each side of the city, and the city will be made of pure gold. Won't that be beautiful? There will be precious stones all along the city too. There will be bright blue

sapphires. Add drops of blue along the bottom next to the yellow walls. **And there will be pretty purple amethysts** (add purple dots along another side) **and shiny yellow beryl.** Add yellow dots on another side. **And there will also be shimmery green emeralds!** Add green dots along the top inside. **So many wonderful stones to make the foundations! There will be a street of pure gold running through the heavenly city.** Paint a yellow street along the top portion inside the wall. **And wait until you see the river of the water of life! True blue and** flowing right through the city. Paint a blue river running across the picture. Add a bit of water to make it shimmery. Then say: **On either side of the river will grow the trees of life that will give fruit every month of the year!** Paint two green trees on either side of the river.

But that's not all. The best is yet to come! Did you know there will never be the dark of night in this city? And guess who will live with us there? God and Jesus will sit on thrones and will rule as kings. Add two large yellow pools of color to the picture. **They will shine bright as day, and we'll never need lamps. God and Jesus will rule as kings forever and ever! Yes!**

Pause a moment, then turn off the overhead projector. Have children sit up, then ask:
● **Why do you think heaven will be a wonderful place?**
● **How is heaven and its beauty a demonstration of God's love for us?**
Read aloud John 14:2, 3. Say: **Jesus promised that he would prepare a place for us in heaven so we can live with him there forever. When Jesus is our Savior, we can trust we'll live forever with him in heaven. What a wonderful promise! Let's close with a prayer thanking the Lord for the wonderful place he's preparing for us.**

PRAY IT!

Place a clean blank transparency on the overhead projector. Use a marker to draw large billowy clouds on the transparency. Then turn on the overhead projector and read aloud the following from the second half of Luke 10:20: "Rejoice that your names are written in heaven." Say: **When we know, love, and follow Jesus, we know that our names are already written in heaven. Let's take turns writing our names in these clouds to show how glad we are that Jesus is preparing a place for us in heaven.**

When kids' names are written on the transparency, have children sit on their pillows, then pray: **Dear Lord, can anything be as wonderful as the new heaven and earth you're making for us? We thank you for your love and care and for the place you make for us here as well as in heaven. We love you! Amen.**

Remind children to take their heavenly headrests home and use them at night to remind them of how wonderful heaven will be. Encourage kids to thank God in advance for the wonderful place he's preparing for us and for his awesome love while we're still on earth.

REPLAY IT!

To reinforce and enrich today's lesson, try one of these fun ideas!

● Let children read Revelation 21:10-21 and 22:1-5. Then spread a 6-foot length of white shelf paper on the floor and turn children loose creating their impression of what the heavenly city will be like. Provide markers, crayons, glitter glue, sequins, fake jewels, foil, glue, and gold wrapping paper to embellish their project.

● Kids will enjoy making heavenly key chains or bracelets. Provide gold satin cord and various fake jewel-type beads in shimmery colors. Use blue, green, rose, red, purple, and turquoise colored beads. As children work, talk about the types of stones that will be used in the foundation of the new Jerusalem. Tie knots in the ends of the cord to prevent the beads from slipping off, then tie the strings around wrists or shoelaces, or use them as backpack key chains to remind kids of the home we'll have in heaven.

Gift Box Pattern

Photocopy and enlarge the pattern. Cut out the pattern along the solid lines.

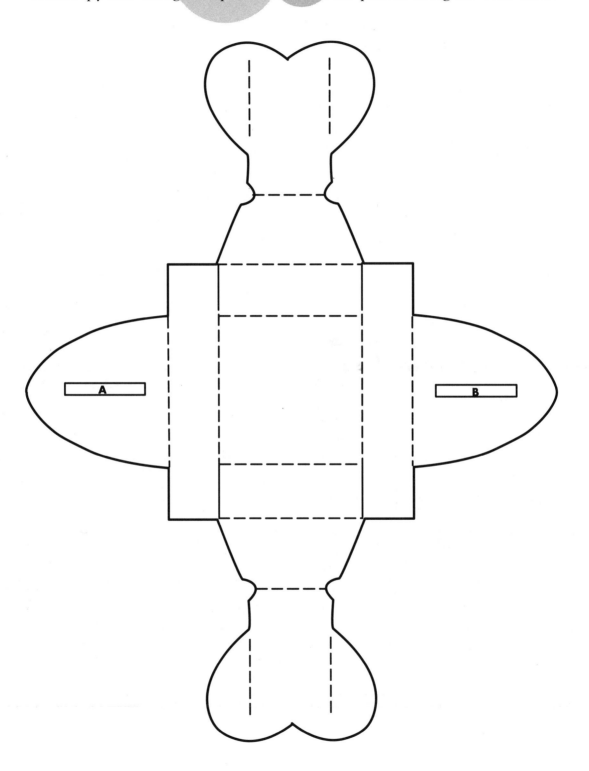

DISCIPLE ID CARDS

Photocopy the cards and cut them out.

Simon
Occupation: Fisherman
Facts: Later renamed Peter by Jesus; one of Jesus' three closest friends

Andrew
Occupation: Fisherman
Facts: Brother of Peter; name means "manly" or "courageous one"

James
Occupation: Fisherman
Facts: Brother of John; called a "Son of Thunder" by Jesus

John
Occupation: Fisherman
Facts: One of Jesus' three closest friends; wrote the Gospel of John

Matthew
Occupation: Tax collector
Facts: Also know as Levi; wrote the Gospel of Matthew

Philip
Occupation: Unknown
Facts: The first disciple Jesus directly called; came from same town as Peter

Thomas
Occupation: Unknown
Facts: Name means "the twin"; at first, he doubted Jesus' resurrection

Bartholomew
Occupation: Unknown
Facts: Later became a missionary; may have died preaching the gospel

Simon
Occupation: Unknown
Facts: Also known as "Simon the Zealot"

James
Occupation: Unknown
Facts: Also known as "James the Younger"; may have been Jesus' cousin

Thaddaeus
Occupation: Unknown
Facts: Later became a missionary telling people about Jesus

Judas
Occupation: Unknown
Facts: Betrayed Jesus for 30 pieces of silver

GOOD SAMARITAN SILHOUETTES

Photocopy and enlarge the patterns, then cut out each figure.